Changing Ministry in Changing Times

Changing Ministry in Changing Times

Tony P. Lane

Foreword by David M. Griffis

Pathway Press

Book Editor: Wanda Griffith
Editorial Assistant: Tammy Hatfield
Copy Editors: Esther Metaxas
Cresta Shawver
Oreeda Burnette
Inside Layout: Mark Shuler

Library of Congress Catalog Card Number: 00-101815
ISBN:0-87148-214-2

Dedication

- To my dad, who prayed for me daily prior to his death, and whose prayers continue to live in the "golden bowls full of incense," as recorded in Revelation 5:8. His walk with God truly exemplified qualities of a member of the contemporary hall of faith. Though he touched many lives, I am greatly indebted for his touch on my life.
- To my mother, who encouraged me, guided me and exemplified godly living during times of great change. Even in the greatest trials in her life as a pastor's wife, her faith never wavered.
- To my wife, Joy, who has been a source of joy to me through many changes in our life together. Because of her encouragement and unfailing love, this project became a reality.
- To my son, Josh, who chose to walk in the way God has directed him for such a time as this. I believe in you, son.
- To my daughter, Meagan, who is a special blessing to the Lane family because of her love for God and the worship she gives Him.
- To Bill Rayburn, a mentor, guide and friend, who introduced me to cross-cultural ministry and the way to handle change in that setting.

CONTENTS

FOREWORD

Changing Ministry in Changing Times resounds the pulse beat of this age—we cannot "do business as usual" by depending on the methods that worked in the past and expect the same results.

In this important work, Tony Lane addresses the many needs of the church that have developed as a result of the changing culture, advanced technology and the pace of the information age. He believes that the message of Jesus Christ and Hid redeeming grace and power in the lives of the people is the most relevant message for these time.

Tony is able in his book to show how we can introduce new methods of ministry without ever changing the power of the message. The son of a Church of God pastor, Tony has served as a successful pastor and youth and Christian education director. He has traveled extensively as a popular teacher and trainer in the field of Sunday school and Christian education. He is aware of the needs of the "changing church" and has written this insightful book to assist church leaders in reaching the lost, not only in "all the world," but also in their own families. He believes we must pass the torch of the gospel from generation to generation, as well as to the unreached masses.

Tony shares with the reader how it is possible to reach a variety of generations—the Seniors, the Boomers, the Busters, the Builders and the Mosaics—with the life-changing message of redemption and discipleship. While the message has never changed, the methodology must change to meet the changing demands of the hour.

As you read this book, you will uncover the following practical and helpful guidelines:

- Evaluations for church structures, programs and curriculum
- Up-to-date familial demographics
- Recruiting principles in the 21st century
- Leadership team interview questions
- Blending generations in praise and worship
- Enhancing family focus in your ministry

These are not just theoretical jargon—they really work! May God anoint and tune your heart and mind for the wonderful things you are about to receive.

—David Griffis
International Director of
Youth and Christian Education
Church of God
Cleveland, Tennessee

Acknowledgments

A book like this can never be written without the influence, help and guidance of many people. As a Church of God preacher's son, I consider myself a product of the church. My views, faith and life have been shaped by laity in churches where my dad served as pastor, as well as by the leaders of our denomination. I have been taught by instructors at Lee University and Wheaton College. God used many individuals to mold my thinking and writing. I offer special gratitude, first to God for His inspiration and guidance. Special appreciation and thanks to:

David Griffis, John Childers and the General Board of Youth and Christian Education for encouraging me and giving me the opportunity to pursue this project.

Tom Madden, a dreamer, a true friend, who encouraged me to color outside the lines.

David Ray, a team player who works with great diligence.

Tony Garcia, a brother who has provided the opportunity for me to share the message of the need for change among the Hispanic constituency.

Daniel Vassell, a friend who has extended his hand.

The International Youth and Christian Education Department staff, a wonderful team to work with. I appreciate your long-suffering spirit and attitude.

Dan Boling and *Bill George*, whose leadership at Pathway Press is providing innovative and creative ministry.

Wanda Griffith for your expertise as the editor of this project.

Wayne Slocumb for a superb cover design. God has indeed gifted you with creativity.

Pat Bradbury and the marketing team for their diligence and hard work in promoting this book. Your friendship is such a blessing.

Sherrie Richardson, my secretary, for her patience and understanding while I was writing this book.

Bill Sowle, my friend, who prayed for me during this process.

INTRODUCTION

The Wonderful Wizard of Oz is the story of Dorothy and her dog, Toto, from Kansas. One night, while Dorothy is sleeping, a tornado picks up her house, spins it around and drops it in a new place. When she wakes up and looks around, she sees a very different picture than what she saw before the tornado. After looking around, she says "Toto, we're not in Kansas anymore."

Those who work in the church understand that we don't live, work or minister in the same world our parents and grandparents did. Growing up in a preacher's home has been an enlightening experience for me. It gave me the opportunity to observe various reactions to change. There were some in each church Dad pastored who longed for change. There were also those who preferred the traditional way of doing things and longed for the "good ole' days." They had difficulty accepting any new ideas.

When I think about the "good ole' days," I recall the stories I've heard from my grandparents. Those were the days of starting the automobile from the outside, no matter what the weather; heating with wood-burning stoves; talking on party-line telephones; and hand-washing clothes on a scrub board. What could be good about the old days?

Those of us who like change must also be cautious that our motivation for change is not just a dissatisfaction with the present. We see in change an answer for the void we are experiencing.

As the need for change is evaluated, it is imperative that we understand the truth that the church, and all it stands for, belongs to God alone. He has established the church and will keep it. Our purpose is to become vessels He can use to make disciples and reap the harvest.

To make an impact in a changing society, we must consider changing some of our methods, not simply for the sake of change, but because God has given His vision and mission to us. This requires flexibility on our part to be open to change and give careful evaluation to know what to change and what to leave the same.

I'm reminded of the story about the mother who was preparing the holiday meal for her family. As she cut the ends off the ham and placed it in the pan, her daughter inquired, "Mom, why do you cut the ends off of the ham before you cook it?" Her mother responded, "That's the way Grandma did it and I've always tried to follow her example." The daughter continued with inquisitive thinking. "Let's call Grandma and ask her why she cut off the ends of the ham." They called Grandma and asked her why she prepared her ham in this manner. She responded, "I cut the ends of my ham before I cooked it because I only had one pan and that's the only way I could make the ham fit in the pan."

For one generation, the only way to make it work was to cut the ham. Out of tradition, the second generation followed this model, without a legitimate reason or even asking why. When the third generation became inquisitive, the original purpose was revealed. Cutting the ends off the ham no longer had validity, but had the question not been asked, the tradition would have continued.

We continue to do things the way we've always done them with the mistaken notion that it's the only way to be effective. If we are to be successful in the ministry to which God has called us, we must address the following questions:

- Am I tired of the status quo?
- Do I really want to reap the harvest?
- Can I handle things differently?

John 21 records a pertinent story. After the resurrection of Jesus, some of the disciples decided to go fishing. They fished the entire night and caught nothing. In the morning, they heard the voice of the Master as He inquired, "Friends, have you caught any fish?" To their negative response, He directed them, "Throw out your net on the right-hand side of the board, and you'll get plenty of fish!" (*NLT*).

I can imagine some of their discussion. Perhaps Thomas at first responded with, "It won't work. We've never done it that way before." Nathaniel may have spoken up. "Yeah, and who is He to tell us how to fish. We've got the experience. We know the trade." Peter joins in. "Doesn't He know that we are fishermen? We're the ones who know how to catch fish successfully." Thomas may have shouted, "We're tired, cold and hungry. We need some rest. We're all burned out. It just must not be God's will for us to catch any fish this time. We'll go back out later, after we eat and get some rest."

The Bible doesn't record any questions or hesitation on their part. Instead, John 21:6 reads, "So they did, and they couldn't draw in the net because there were so many fish in it" (*NLT*).

They didn't respond in fear, they responded in faith. I believe they recognized the voice of the Master Fisherman. In obedience to the plan He gave them, they reaped a great harvest. The key is obeying His directive.

Some churches are involved in meaningful activities. Many well-meaning people are working in local vineyards, but they are seeing little progress. It's not time to work harder. Rather, it's time we work smarter, because He promised us, "My yoke is easy, and my burden is light" (Matthew 11:30).

Recently I read a story in *Who Moved My Cheese?* by Spencer Johnson. The author relates the parable of two mice and two little people who live in a maze. They are looking for cheese to nourish them and make them happy. The little people's names are Hem and Haw. The mice are named Sniff and Scurry. Cheese is a metaphor for receiving satisfaction in life. In the story, the characters assume the daily task of going after the cheese. Once they learn the route, their daily routine becomes quite simple. However, one day they follow the same routine, expecting the same results and find that someone has moved the cheese. Each character deals with this sudden and unexpected change differently. The moral of the story is that change happens and it needs to be anticipated.

When change is expected, it becomes easier to let go of the old and accept the new. For those not satisfied with the status quo, the new and different is an adventure waiting to happen!

Change is difficult, but we must expect it and deal with it. In fact, we must plan for it. Seek the face of God. Climb on board for the ride of your life!

There is an old saying that the things that got you to where you are today are not the things that will get you to where you need to be tomorrow.

George Barna, *The Second Coming of the Church*

Changing Ministry

1

From the tribe of Issachar, there were 200 leaders of the tribe with their relatives. All these men understood the temper of the times and knew the best course for Israel to take.

1 Corinthians 12:32, NLT

Growing up in a pastor's home gave me an opportunity to observe a variety of church models and ministries. I had the privilege of meeting people from various walks of life. Some were diligent in their work for God . . . others served God recklessly, without a strong commitment. In some churches the constituents were mainly farmers, while other congregations were made up of members who were in upper-level management. Some of these congregations experienced great growth; others saw temporary growth, followed by a return to the "old guard."

Resistance to Change

Change in each of these situations was often difficult. Even though my dad was very good in his role of change agent, often the congregation was not receptive to the change. "We've never done it that way before," was the excuse given by church members, committees and pastor's councils. Sometimes, that phrase would negate the possibility of change. At other times, some brave soul would challenge the thinking and invite those involved to open their minds for critical consideration of the suggested change.

I sometimes wonder if the singer of the song, "Give Me That Old-Time Religion," might have been expressing more about religious tradition and even opposition to change, rather than to a walk of faith. I remember some of the most glorious services were when the church sang the lyrics to that familiar gospel song. Its theme reflected some Christians' attitudes toward change. They saw change as inherently evil and perceived that God was angry when He initiated change among His people or in His work. They wanted to hold to the tradition of past experiences.

In one church it was suggested that the name be changed to reflect the community where the church was now located, rather than the community where it was originally planted. When the pastor suggested the possibility of renaming the church to reflect the new location, some members of the congregation considered this blasphemous and became enraged at the suggestion. Even though the church no longer resided in its original location, there were people who desired to hold on to the original name because it identified a specific place and time in their past. Little did they understand that the simple name change would be welcomed by the community and would perhaps open new doors of ministry. The past identity was more important to them than any progress that might come with the change. My dad, who had great discernment, understood that it wasn't worth the battle and opted to forgo the name change.

In a rapidly changing world, the church must also be willing to change if it continues to be effective in its ministry. This is where the tension lies. The Bible is filled with absolutes that serve as our constant guide. The Word of God is changeless, but the body of Christ requires change.

Growth Brings Change

A student of the Word understands that in the Books of Ephesians and 1 Corinthians, the writer describes the church as a living, growing organism. In order to be healthy, everybody must grow. Therefore, with growth comes change. It is necessary!

Some people are constantly changing things in their lives so that nothing remains constant. Others rarely, if ever, move the furniture in their living room or bedroom. They find comfort in the familiar, so they adjust to the traditional.

Many of our practices and programs are simply part of church tradition and are not necessarily bad. However, if we search for a Biblical basis for these practices, we will not likely find any. For example, Sunday school is not mentioned in the Bible. Neither are youth programs, midweek services, church membership or even church nurseries. When we evaluate our traditions, we must understand that changing these traditions should not be equated with changing our doctrinal stance.

Evaluate Ministry Programs

As we look at our society, we see great change. Changing demographics require us to evaluate our present structures and programs to accommodate adequate ministry.

"The teen population is expected to grow at twice the rate of the rest of the population during the next decade, peaking in 2080 with approximately 30.8 million teenagers. This is 900,000 more teens than ever before. In fact, it's 4.1 million more than in 1969 when Woodstock woke up mainstream America to youth culture's existence."[1]

What does this mean as we evaluate our local church ministry program? Should we continue conducting business as usual? How should this influence the local church budget? Where should our emphases lie?

On the other hand, George Barna has discovered that the probability of accepting Christ is highest among kids under 14 years of age. The data from Barna's survey, shared on *Barna Research Online*, shows that children ages 5 through 13 have a 32 percent probability of accepting Christ as their Savior. Teens ages of 14 through 18 have just a 4 percent likelihood, while adults, ages 19 and above, have only a 6 percent probability of making that choice. With this in mind, the church must evaluate the possibility of ministry shifts.

We have seen a shift from the culture to a diverse culture. As various cultural groups invade communities, new ministry opportunities arise. However, we must evaluate our current ministry by asking these questions:

- Will the church be open to individuals from other cultures?
- Are there walls of prejudice that must be torn down?
- How does the congregation become sensitive to multicultural ministry opportunities?
- Should a Spanish-speaking service be added?
- Would a diversified music style help break down other barriers?

Multicultural ministry requires a diversified strategy that must be dealt with very carefully.

With the great variety of changes coming in the third millennium, churches should ask the question, Are we effectively reaching the lost and effectively discipling those whom we win? Is the church seeing numerical and spiritual growth? If not, it's time for change! Just as every individual is born with a destiny, so is every church and every ministry. Why did God place you where you are? Because He trusts you to make a difference. This often requires becoming instruments of change.

It is time for us to make a difference! As church leaders, we must ask ourselves,

- Are we leading effectively?
- Should we consider doing things differently?
- Isn't it time to step outside the box and color outside the lines?

The world is looking for a church that is alive and relevant. Jesus went to where the people were and preached a message they could understand. His message often went against their traditional teachings. They could not understand the message that God created mankind to live an abundant life. For many, this was in direct opposition to what they were practicing. Therefore, change was necessary.

Paying the Price

Once we have decided to change, we must allow God to stretch us, move us out of our comfort zones. The old saying, "No pain, no gain," is true. Without the rough edges, we can never see the smooth places. However, when we pay the price of change through prayer and fasting, we can receive a word from God that is for us personally and for our congregation.

The reason we often have difficulty working through change is because we aren't working through a divine strategy. We may need to change our methods in order to capture the world's attention, but it must start with a word from God!

- What does God want me to do differently?

- When is it going to be done?
- Are my deadlines reasonable?
- Where will we be six months, or a year from now?

If we aim for nothing, we will hit it every time. God's church is a church on the move. God's church does not operate in the status quo!

Satan wants us to be overwhelmed and discouraged. He understands that effective ministry requires change and he will do everything within his power to restrict us and inhibit change. However, we must understand the times and know what we need to do! We also have this assurance: "Greater is he that is in you, than he that is in the world" (1 John 4:4, KJV).

Unless we consciously prepare to move up to the next level of effectiveness, we will remain where we are, often in a rut, doing what we've always done. But God desires to do a new thing. The new thing may be a change in the system or a change in an individual. When a church added adult electives to its Sunday school curriculum, more adults started attending Sunday school. This was a change in the system that worked on behalf of the people.

Impact of Technology

As we enter the 21st century, the rate of change is accelerating. New weather patterns with extended hurricane seasons, violent floods and stage-five tornadoes are rampant. Our methods of communication are changing as we watch the vast expansion of technology. The World Wide Web, automobiles, home appliances and office equipment all promise a quick and easy lifestyle. We live in an age where information is doubling every four years. The amount of information that can be programmed into a computer chip doubles every 18 months. Our society is experiencing "information overload." This has created a generation that resists change, but they desire the unchanging Word of God because it has a relevant message for every generation. We have an obligation to evaluate our ministry so that every generation will have the opportunity to know and live the abundant life.

What a wonderful privilege to continue what Christ began when He told Peter, "Upon this rock I will build my church and the gates of hell shall not prevail against it"(Matthew 16:18). We cannot return to the "good ole' days." Neither can we lose the faithful members who provided the heritage we now enjoy. This is our dilemma!

Building Bridges

As we make necessary changes, it is important to understand that in order to bring about change, we must build a bridge from the past to the future. One vital aspect of the Jewish religion is passing the faith from one generation to the next. Grandparents and parents alike tell stories of important traditions and customs to their children and grandchildren. We too must respect and support the older generation by taking customs and traditions into consideration. Some we will be able to endorse; others may fall by the wayside. But if we bathe the process of change in loving relationships, perhaps we can salvage the pioneers of our faith.

Whoever coined the phrase, "One size fits all," was certainly not talking about the contemporary church. What a challenge we have before us! We have always had diversity of cultures, but never have the lines of diversity been so well defined. We have to address these differences in order to determine what God wants the church to become and how He wants us to minister. What was once considered contemporary is no longer contemporary. When the Willow Creek Community Church, now the largest church in the U.S., started the "seeker style" of ministry in the 1970s, it was perceived as contemporary. However, they are re-evaluating their approach to take into consideration the various differences so visible in our society. What was once considered contemporary language, contemporary worship music, and contemporary styles of worship are no longer meeting the diverse needs of the population.

Our challenge is to enhance our present forms of ministry so that every generation will be accepting and continue to see spiritual growth, regardless of the winds of change. Some will have extreme difficulty accepting revolutionary change. Because they invested a major portion of their lives building the church, it will be difficult to accept anything new. We must be sensitive to the needs of these older adults, while recognizing the needs of a changing society. Therein lies our challenge for changing ministry in changing times!

And now, may the God of peace equip you with all you need for doing His will

(Hebrews 13:20, *NLT*).

We've done our work, carefully unfolding God's spoken Word. Now we pack up our insights into well-chosen phrases and send them out across this nation's pulpits and restaurant tables and neighborhood fences. The perfect gift. But the address of the world around us has changed. Dramatic shifts in the fabric of American culture have nudged the world out of reach of the words we've so carefully selected. . . . The world has moved, but it neglected to send a change of address card. We keep delivering the same words to the old address, but no one is home.

David W. Henderson, *Culture Shift*

One Faith in a Diverse Culture

2

Matthew 5:14-16, TM

You're here to be light, bringing out the God-colors in the world. God is not a secret to be kept. We're going public with this, as public as a city on a hill. If I make you light-bearers, you don't think I'm going to hide you under a bucket, do you? I'm putting you on a light stand. Now that I've put you there on a hilltop, on a light stand shine! Keep open house; be generous with your lives. By opening up to others, you'll prompt people to open up with God, this generous Father in heaven.

I stood gazing at the magnificent structure as it loomed before me. Situated on a lonesome field on the outskirts of town, the temple pointed heavenward. For months, I had read comments, questions and essays in the community newspaper. Great fear gripped the hearts of many. Rumor had it that a Hindu temple would be erected on this swampy land. Who would have thought that Aurora, Illinois, would be the best location? It was a suburban community 40 miles west of Chicago with a Hispanic and African-American population and a rumored Columbian drug connection.

Aurora, "City of Lights," was now the home to a highly unusual house of worship for a unique and diverse congregation. Followers of the Hindu religion came from far and wide for this day of dedication. Tents were erected on the premises to house the gods that would fill the altar areas throughout the temple, as well as placement on the roof of the mighty structure. Gold imported from India covered the dome and sparkled in the bright sun. Fruit, vegetables, flowers and other types of offerings lay at the feet of the man-made gods. Indeed, I felt as if I had been placed in a time machine and transported to a land and culture I had only read about. But, it was only a few blocks from my house, just a few blocks from my church, down the street from the public school and across the way from a new housing development. The culture of India had taken up residence in Aurora, Illinois.

Our Pluralistic Society

Christian education today takes place in a world that is very different from the world in which it was developed. Our society is no longer a monistic society. Rather, it has become pluralistic, because in every community there are many non-Christian groups meeting for worship. Muslim mosques and Hindu temples are prevalent throughout metropolitan areas, as well as in many cities and towns. When traveling through major airports, it is not uncommon to see individuals praying to their respective gods. The dress of their religion is worn proudly, a visible reminder of our pluralistic culture.

The word *pluralism* refers to a society with more than one form of faith. The United States was founded on the principle of freedom of religion. A *monistic* society is one in which there is only one faith to which everyone belongs. The Yellow Pages of the phone book today reveal diverse faiths listed under "churches." We no longer live and work in a monistic society! So then, how should we educate Christians in such a pluralistic environment? What significance does this have for the body of Christ?

Responding to Pluralism

Some would like to revert to the "little white church in the vale." Their preference would be to return to the past and live a separated life within a pluralistic society.

Throughout the United States, there are Amish communities that have tried to segregate themselves and hold on to their belief system. However, we cannot escape the fact that North America is culturally and religiously diverse. This means that instead of going to school with friends from church who are of the same Protestant faith, our children are exposed to teachings, practices and belief systems that we never encountered. This exposure requires a careful response. If we do not teach them how to live and respond to the diversity of cultures, they can be absorbed by it. They may compromise their faith or even desert it. There is a strong need for the church to educate its constituency by addressing the pluralism represented in the community. The first step in this process is acknowledging the situation. Then we must teach our children, and our congregations as a whole, the truth.

Enhancing the Vision

Confronting different belief systems and religious cultures challenges our thinking. Are we teaching our children what they need to know in order to develop a sound faith? Have we become too familiar with what we teach and believe by allowing it to become stagnant in our lives? One challenge in Christian education is to enhance the vision of the familiar. It is our responsibility to make faith come alive to students so that they have not only a head knowledge, but a value system that encompasses their whole being.

We must arouse interest and curiosity again in the eyes of the learner. Today's generation is looking for something new, something meaningful, something nontraditional. Then, when the militant recruiter of the Black Muslims comes looking for prospects, he will leave for lack of interest.

Teaching the Basics

A few years ago, we began to place less emphasis on Sunday school. As a result of this de-emphasis on teaching, we have raised a generation of Biblically illiterate Christians. Our young people have not been taught the basic doctrine and tenets of our faith. They have not had the opportunity to enjoy the small group discipleship and learning that occurs in the

Sunday school ministry setting. Nor have they had anyone to hold them accountable for what they have or have not learned. This lack of Scriptural knowledge has left them in need when confronted with an opposing doctrine or teaching. In other instances, we have failed to advance our teaching style and methodology, thereby expecting students to listen to boring lectures, void of life-giving truth. Then, some revolutionary idea is presented that challenges their thinking and they buy into it because their curiosity has been aroused.

We must also teach our students to respect other belief systems and religions, without endorsing them. In the past, perhaps we were guilty of teaching that our church was the only group of people going to heaven. We must not isolate ourselves and become exclusive in our approach; lest we become like those we are criticizing. I can recall growing up believing that members of my church were the only people going to heaven. All who did not belong to our church were doomed for hell. That became the motivation for evangelism.

Respecting Other Faiths

In order to teach respect and even appreciation for other faiths and religions, we must know what they really believe. Sometimes, false information is passed along about other faiths. We need to carefully study, investigate and evaluate other religions in our community so that we can discuss them intelligently. For example, one of the fears of the residents in Aurora was that the town would be overrun by rats. Someone had shared with the community that people in the Hindu religion believed that rats should never be killed and that they should be permitted to multiply. This fear immediately built walls, which then prevented relationship building and subsequent possibilities for evangelism. We can learn some valuable truths from other faiths in our community.

I recall taking students to the temple to see it and observe the worshipers. As they entered the temple, they learned that they must remove their shoes. Lesson number one was that there was great respect for their house of worship. Lesson number two came when we were welcomed by an individual wearing unique clothing. He looked different, but he extended his hand to us and welcomed us. The students then understood the importance of respecting those who appear different and welcoming them to the sanctuary for worship. Lesson number three was learned as the students observed the offerings being placed at the feet of the golden idols. The worshipers had sacrificed, driven long distances and then brought an offering for their god. Still a fourth lesson came as the students listened to the different style of music, watched the worshipers in their dance and observed the high price that had been paid for the temple.

When we arrived back at the church, we discussed how our exposure to these issues had initiated a learning experience that would have not happened if we had ignored this unique group of people and their house of worship.

A part of this pluralistic society is the opportunity for individuals to pick their god. We have a great responsibility to help them to choose Christ and to show them why He is the only Way, the only Truth. We must give them room to doubt their faith in order for it to grow. Books like Josh McDowell's *Evidence That Demands a Verdict* are a helpful source as students gather evidence to support a faith founded in the Word of God. It is imperative that we train our sons and daughters in the tenets of our faith. It is not enough for them to respond, "I believe it because my church believes it." It must be a personal belief system based not on a denominational stance, but on the Word of God—the cornerstone of our faith!

The Discipleship Process

The advancement of technology and the "information revolution" encourages us as a church to tell our story and pass along our faith. Sometimes young people experiment with new teachings and different views, but this period of questioning is usually temporary as they seek to "work out [their] own salvation with fear and trembling" (Philippians 2:12). Adults coming from various backgrounds will take the teaching and evaluate it through the traditions of their own cultural background.

The best we can do is provide quality discipleship training that will protect them from false doctrine. Teaching by example is a vital part of this discipleship process. Individuals must learn how to apply the Word daily in their lives. As they watch others, they will learn how to be Christian in thought, word and deed. This observation enables learners to grow and become more Christlike.

As we move into the third millennium, mentoring becomes a major emphasis of Christian education. Christ provided an example for us to follow. When He began His ministry, He chose a group of disciples to walk alongside Him, observing all that He did. Throughout His ministry, He assisted them and encouraged them as He prepared them for future ministry. There are other examples of mentoring in the New Testament. Paul regularly took disciples along with him on his missionary journeys. Luke and Timothy were both recipients of Paul's teaching and guidance.

Curriculum Selection

One of the greatest tasks of living in a diverse culture is training believers so that their faith grows to maturity. If we do not do a better job at "growing up" believers, we will continue to run the risk of losing them to other churches. Equipping the believer is critical to retaining new converts. George Barna, in his book, *Second Coming of the Church*, makes the following statement:

> A majority of those who make a decision for Christ wander away from the church within eight weeks of making such a decision. This is largely because no one disciples or mentors those individuals as to the meaning and application of their newly embraced faith. The

> result is that many who make a decision never become true converts, and may be spiritually crippled for life, thinking they have mastered Christianity when, in fact, they have merely taken the first step down the road of faith.[1]

A carefully selected curriculum with a scope and sequence that can be easily followed will assist the local church in making sure the learners are getting a Biblical foundation. When local church workers select their own curriculum, many times there is a hodgepodge of teaching that has no continuity or flow for the overall Christian education program. Because of the variety of teaching materials available, all curriculum materials should be evaluated and screened by the local Christian education board or committee. An even better strategy would be to incorporate an overall curriculum plan for the entire church. Otherwise, some Biblical teaching may be left out.

As a local Christian education director, I recall receiving samples of children's church curriculum that came highly recommended. After reviewing it, we learned that it taught the children how to speak in tongues as they sought the experience of the Baptism of the Holy Spirit. Included on the visuals were syllables to teach the children as they prayed for the experience. Since this was in total disagreement with our doctrinal stance, we immediately decided against the curriculum.

Never before have we been bombarded with so many choices and styles of teaching materials. It would be wise for us to carefully consider all options and see how they fit in the overall master plan of training and Christian education in our church.

Another consideration for curriculum selection and evaluation is whether or not it reflects the cultural and ethnic identity of the learner. As we endeavor to teach respect for diversity, we should make sure the materials being used in the Christian education setting reflect these concerns:

- Does the curriculum address the cultural needs of the students?
- Does the curriculum address the need for a personal relationship with Jesus Christ?
- Is the curriculum Biblically based?
- Does the doctrine taught in the curriculum line up with the Word of God and with the teachings of our faith?

As we embrace the idea of building relationships with those who are different from us and come from a different culture than ours, flexibility will be a key ingredient. While we acknowledge the differences, we must continue to build on the foundation of the Word of God, a plumb line by which everything else is evaluated. If our teaching resources do not match what the Word of God is teaching, then we must reevaluate. If the resources do not help us become more effective disciples, growing and maturing in the faith, then they are not what we need.

Yes, in this pluralistic society, God's divine appointment may be an individual raised in the

Hindu culture or in the Muslim faith. Hopefully, the church to which I ascribe has prepared or is preparing me to be salt and light for the world that has arrived at my back door.

> *Let me tell you why you are here. You're here to be salt-seasoning that brings out the God-flavors of this earth. If you lose your saltiness, how will people taste godliness? You've lost your usefulness and will end up in the garbage*
> **(Matthew 5:13, TM).**

If we do not change direction, we are likely to end up where we are headed.

Ancient Chinese Proverb

Ministering Through Children

3

Matthew 19:13, NLT

Some children were brought to Jesus so he could lay his hands on them and pray for them. The disciples told them not to bother him. But Jesus said, "Let the children come to me. Don't stop them! For the Kingdom of Heaven belongs to such as these." And he put his hands on their heads and blessed them before he left.

From the time Jesus established the New Testament church, He gave primary importance to children. At a time in Biblical history when women and children did not enjoy the same social status as men, Jesus affirmed their role. Jesus gave significance to a child who gave his meager lunch to feed thousands. And it was Jesus who reminded us that unless we become as little children in our faith, we will never see the kingdom of God. Jesus valued children.

Children's Ministry

It is time to evaluate the way we minister to children whose lives have been shattered by change. Fractured families and broken children comprise our communities, as well as our churches. In his book, *The Index of Leading Cultural Indicators*, William J. Bennett points out that between 1960 and 1998, the percentage of single-parent families more than tripled. Single-parent families comprise 31.7 percent of all families in the United States. He also alerts us to the fact that 64 percent of these single-parent families are black, 35 percent are Hispanic, and 32 percent are white. Of the more than 71 million children in the United States, almost one-third do not live in a two-parent family.[1] What does that mean to us in the changing church? Are we effectively ministering to these single-parent children and their parents? Do we understand the implications if we don't?

Bennett also refers to the following statistics from the National Center for Health Statistics:

- During the 1990s, the number of cohabiting households increased by almost 50 percent.
- One of every six children is a stepchild.
- In 1980, there were 431,000 households with unmarried couples with children under 15 years of age; in 1997, there were 1,470,000.
- The odds that a child today will witness the divorce of his or her parents are one in two. A generation ago, the odds were one in four.

- The number of children involved in divorce was 463,000 in 1980, but rose to 1.05 million in 1995.
- Children whose parents are divorced are more likely to exhibit conduct problems, psychological maladjustment and lower academic achievement. They are also more likely to drop out of school, engage in premarital sex and become pregnant ouside of marriage, compared to children in intact families.
- Between 1990 and 1996, the percentage of children in poverty stayed about the same. Overall, between 1970 and 1996, the percentage of children in poverty increased by one-third. Children in poverty are related children in families with an annual income below the poverty level. According to the U.S. Department of Commerce in 1997, the poverty level was $16,400 per year for a family of four.
- Almost one out of every five children in America lives in poverty.
- In 1997, there were 3 million reports of child abuse and neglect—more than double 1986's 1.4 million reports.
- Children whose parents abuse drugs and alcohol are almost three times more likely to be physically or sexually assaulted and more than four times likelier to be neglected than children of parents who are not substance abusers.[2]

Yes, children's ministry has changed. Why? Because the needs have changed. According to Shelly

Cunningham, quoted in "Children's Ministry in Changing Times" in *Sundoulos*, the following needs to be considered:

Fifty years ago, the top seven problems in public schools were (1) talking, (2) chewing gum, (3) making noise, (4) running in the halls, (5) getting out of line, (6) wearing improper clothes, and (7) not putting paper in the wastebasket. Today, the top seven problems are (1) drug abuse, (2) alcohol abuse, (3) pregnancy, (4) suicide, (5) rape, (6) robbery, and (7) assault.[3]

We have children who are harboring a lot of guilt, anguish, fear and shame. They have been abused, neglected and pushed aside. Their parents are living stress-filled lives as a result of trying to live the American dream. Children are forced to deal with divorced parents or no parents. They live in a world that teaches them the humanistic philosophy that only the strong survive. They are babysitters for their siblings and caretakers for their parents. Frequently, they are being diagnosed with attention deficit disorder (ADD) and prescribed stimulant drugs to help them cope. Bennett reports in his book that nearly 4 million children are now taking Ritalin—more than twice the number in 1990.[4]

Specialized Training

Effective ministry to children today goes far beyond babysitting. It involves much more than serving cookies, juice and a flannelgraph story.

Those who minister to children today must be willing to take risks as they reach out to battered souls. Children's ministry workers deserve specialized training as they endeavor to touch a generation that has different needs. In order to meet those needs, the teacher needs to get to know each child and then adjust the curriculum and program accordingly. We can't afford to waste time teaching an irrelevant lesson with so many needy children sitting at our feet!

I grew up in a church where everyone looked alike and spoke the same language. That is no longer the rule. Churches that enjoy successful children's ministry in the 21st century understand, acknowledge and value the diversity in their ministry. Children are not second-class citizens. The trend in public education today is for parents to choose the school their children will attend. Many parents desire a school where their children will be appropriately cared for. They are also looking for a church that cares for children. It is important for children to feel a part of the church. As churches decide to aggressively pursue a caring attitude toward children, they may want to consider the following attributes of a child-friendly church:

- *All children are welcome here.* This can be accomplished by providing children who serve as greeters to welcome children when they walk in. A visitor's packet for children can be presented at the same time the adult visitor's packets are distributed. A welcome center for children, staffed by children and children's workers can be located in the lobby or hallway. Pictures of children in the children's ministry can be displayed appropriately on the walls or bulletin boards in the hallway or vestibule areas.

- *Meet the needs of each child.* Teaching approaches will vary, dependent upon the makeup of the learners in the class. It is important that the teacher understand that every child is different, unique and must be reached individually. The needs of children are varied and will have to be met in a variety of ways.
- *Accommodate special-needs children.* Jesus exemplified this when He stopped to assist those in need. Sometimes, the individual was blind; other times deaf. Still other times, the person was crippled or lonely. Extra staff may be required to assist with those who have special needs. Often, they require one-on-one assistance. Let's do our best to provide the needed help! Teachers need to be trained to teach children with special needs. The curriculum may need adapting so that it is relative and appropriate.
- *Recognize the children.* They love to be acknowledged. This can be done both privately and corporately. Display their work for all to see; call their names publicly; hang pictures of children in the room. Look for ways to recognize

every child. Some children never have the pleasure of being encouraged by a friend, teacher, sibling or parent. We have been called to be ministers of encouragement!

Children's Involvement

To provide quality ministry for children, the children need to be included in the life of the local church. This is accomplished by acknowledging that . . .

- Children are important.
- Children can minister.
- Children need to be taught.
- Children can worship.

Using children in the various ministries of the church encourages them to develop their gifts, talents and abilities. It also provides training and discipleship opportunities. Children can also lead in worship. When children's church was introduced several years ago, the curriculum offered was usually an extension of Sunday school. Their target audience was usually through the sixth grade. However, as children begin to mature earlier, the time has come for us to consider the fact that children can worship. They don't need someone to babysit them while their parents enjoy the worship service. They don't just need games and refreshments. Children need to be a part of the worship service.

I recall my early experience as a young children's church director. My dad appointed me to the position shortly after I began teaching Sunday school at age 12. My goal at that time was to involve the junior church in a worship service that was geared to their needs. I had one of the men in the church build a short pulpit, along with short altar benches. (I believed strongly about the importance of praying in the altar and wanted to encourage the children to do so.) I arranged the room with two sections of chairs and an aisle down the middle. Each week, different children were assigned the responsibility of various aspects of the service. A few years ago, a mother told me that her daughter never forgot her experience in that children's church. It had a profound impact on her life until she died of cancer in her early 20s.

Too often, children have been sent to a room somewhere to be kept busy while their parents enjoy a real service in the main sanctuary. We have done a lot of disservice to children and parents by this method of operation and programming. With the necessary training, children can be used as ushers and greeters. They can sing and pray. Children's church can be the training ground for each of these ministry aspects.

At a recent national children's ministries convention, an evangelist illustrated the faith of a child. He and his staff train and take children on short-term missions trips. On one such excursion, a 10-year-old girl came to him and asked permission to go and pray for a lady in the service who was seated in a wheel chair. He affirmed her faith and encouraged her to do what she believed God wanted her to do. Through her obedience, and because of her faith, God healed the crippled woman. Perhaps that is what Christ was referring to when He told us that unless we have the faith of a little child, we can't inherit the kingdom of God.

Evangelistic Window

Children's ministry also needs to be a priority in the church budget. I stated in chapter 1 that George Barna's survey revealed that the probability of accepting Christ is highest among kids under 14 years of age. Based on his survey, people ages 5 through 13 have a 32 percent probability of accepting Christ as their Savior, while there is only 10 percent probability for those beyond 13 years of age. This study clearly notes that the greatest evangelistic window currently available is among young children. Therefore, there needs to be a greater investment of money, time and energy where it will make perhaps the greatest impact. Perhaps we could save ourselves a lot of work and trouble in youth ministry if we would focus more on ministry to children.

Setting Priorities

Some of this investment will need to be made in facilities that are child-friendly. It's not what you have, but it's what you do with what you have. An evaluation of the local church facilities will reveal where the real needs for improvement lie. A visit by the children's ministry team to the local elementary school will show them what children are using in their classrooms daily. Investment in computers and software, video players, video cameras, CD players, overhead projectors, video projectors and other electronic technology will demonstrate to the local congregation and the community that children's ministry is a priority!

Safety is also an issue that must be considered as we look at the changing needs of children. Parents must be convinced that their children are safe in the care of your church. In *Ministries Today*, author David Middlebrook says:

> Each year, parents, guardians or others seriously abuse approximately 2 million children throughout the U.S. Every year, at least 1,000 children will die as a result of abust and neglect. Some 90 percent of deaths resulting from abuse or neglect involved children under the age of 5; 44 percent of deaths involve children under the age of 1. These statistics do not take into account thousands of unreported acts of child abuse.[5]

This causes great fear and anxiety on the part of many church leaders today. Much of the anxiety is due to the devastation involved when an individual is accused of child abuse. Many wise churches have developed a screening program for those who work with children. Hopefully, this will relieve some of the fear and anxiety. The purpose of the screening program is for prospective workers to reveal if they have ever been convicted of abuse. With such a transient population, we really don't always know the newcomers in our church. Jesus exhorted us to be careful and wise. This is one area where we need to improve. Background checks have become necessary in many cases. Middlebrook has also developed a program for churches to help prevent child abuse—STOP.

- **S**creen everyone who has contact with children and teens from pastors, teacher and children's workers to volunteers.
- **T**rain the responsible people in children's, youth and teen ministry, from leaders to workers (paid or volunteer), how to prevent child abuse and follow reporting guidelines.
- **O**perate the STOP program effectively in the church.
- **P**lan to immediately report and handle any suspected child abuse. (The STOP program is available from Charisma Life Publishers. For information, call 800-451-4598.)

If we are going to protect our children by offering care and safety; if we desire to avoid legal bills; if we provide staff members who are without risk to others; if we don't have funds to lose, we have no choice. We must do everything we can to prevent child abuse in our ministry.

The task of offering effective children's ministry in today's world is challenging. In the past, local churches survived with a children's worker whose primary focus was Sunday school and perhaps Vacation Bible School. This individual was rarely paid and not viewed as a primary player on the ministry team. Changing times require changing models.

Effective children's ministries today include individuals who have accepted the specialized challenges of today's children in an extremely complex world. Often the position includes ministry to families, a paradigm that is now shifting. Continual pleas for workers should be a reminder that children's ministry is one of the greatest needs and priorities of ministry today. Even if it is only a part-time position, a children's pastor needs to be considered. It must be seen as a integral and vital ingredient for the church's ministry to children in need. Together with the youth pastor, a children's ministry team can be developed that will make a dramatic difference in holistic ministry to the family. This team effort will serve today's families who perceive extra commitments as a threat to their time together. One of the changes that must be considered is the threat parents perceive emerging from the church. They are becoming very protective of the time they spend as a family. And, because of the many commitments of various family members to job, education, and other extracurricular activities, time spent in church is often where the cut comes.

Since 1985 the number of babies born each year has been increasing by 100,000 a year, and the birth rate exceeded that of 1950, which was a high point during the baby-boom years. These children will be coming to our churches! Are we ready?

And He will turn the hearts of the fathers to the children, and the hearts of the children to their fathers

(Malachi 4:6, *NKJV*).

Qualifications of a Children's Pastor in Changing Times*

- *Dependency on God.* The abilities are important, but greater is the reliance upon what God wants in the children's ministry.
- *People person.* We must have a leader with a servant's heart. The individual must not be independent in spirit and attitude, but able to work alongside the rest of the staff, both paid and volunteer.
- *Lover of children.* Hopefully, the leader will have experience in children's ministry from other situations.
- *Sound marriage.* If married, a sound marriage with a positive relationship with his/her spouse is a must.
- *Self-sacrificing.* A children's pastor should be willing to work without complaining; willing to go the extra mile.
- *Submissive toward pastoral leadership.* A children's pastor cannot be easily offended.
- *Spiritual maturity.* Strong knowledge of the Word is vital! This reflects the fruit of the Spirit and a godly lifestyle.
- *Flexible.* A good leader works well under pressure, doesn't run from problems, but is willing to work through them, especially personality conflicts.
- *Optimistic and positive mind-set.* He or she cannot be critical of leadership, nor one to talk about it.

- *Respected.* Not only by the main church body, but especially by the senior pastor and those with whom he/she will work.
- *Hungry for God.* A children's pastor must be a praying person, committed to the Lord's leading.
- *Self-starter.* An individual who is able to get started on a project without having to be told.
- *Communicates.* Someone who plans with a supervisor prior to initiating those plans.
- *Faithful in stewardship.* A children's pastor must be a giver, a tither and a financially responsible person.
- *Physically fit.* A leader should be disciplined and in good health—able to work long hours when needed without complaining.
- *Proven track record.* Past experience speaks for the leader.
- *Teachable.* Someone who is willing to learn, receive advice and is approachable makes a good leader.
- *Learner.* Good leaders look for resources to further prepare for more effective ministry. They are willing to attend conferences and seminars, as well as training classes.
- *Leader.* Good leaders have leadership qualifications and are perceived as leaders by their peers.
- *Teacher.* Someone who is able to train others; disciple-maker. These leaders are creative, willing to try various teaching methods.

*These characteristics are not listed in order of importance or priority.

"No one tears a piece of cloth from a new garment and uses it to patch an old garment. For then the new garment would be torn, and the patch wouldn't even match the old garment. And no one puts new wine into old wineskins. The new wine would burst the old skins, spilling the wine and ruining the skins. New wine must be put into new wineskins. But no one who drinks the old wine seems to want the fresh and the new. 'The old is better,' they say."

Jesus, Luke 5:36-39, *NLT*

Identifying With Youth Ministry

4

One generation passes away,
and another generation comes.

Ecclesiastes 1:4, NKJV

My first exposure to youth ministry was when I was in the first grade. A member of the Boomer generation, I was born to parents who belonged to the Builder generation. My mother was a faithful worker in her local church, serving as president of the Young People's Endeavor (YPE). She prepared weekly programs that involved the teenagers. Often, she planned a social gathering of some sort. That's the part I recall; a hobo party at our house where everyone dressed as hobos and ate out of soup cans. There were "happy days," playing games, having a great time and enjoying being together. Those were the days of sock hops, bobby socks, white T-shirts and blue jeans and poodle skirts.

Then, time marched on and I became a teenager. It was a different time in a different place among a new generation. Young People's Endeavor (YPE), the midweek service, was replaced with an emphasis on fun and having a good time. Vices in the so-called world were vying for the attention of the youth in the church. Everything possible was done to protect and isolate the teens from negative influence. Parents lived together. Schools had dress codes and maintained discipline. Then, it happened. I remember the day when the school board met and addressed the dress code issue. The entire student body walked out of their classrooms to support a more liberated dress code, allowing girls to wear pants to school.

Change comes and along with it new issues emerge, some complex and others simple.

Changing Values

Shortly thereafter, the youth culture exploded across America. With rock music came Woodstock and "free love." Television came on the scene and the world came into the home. No longer could the youth be barred from all the world had to offer. New problems surfaced: sexual immorality, drugs and drinking. These vices appealed to the youth as the "American dream" played out before them through the media. For the first time, they were exposed to life's many attractions. No longer was their hunger satisfied by popcorn, hayrides and softball games. This hunger grew for things of the world and all Satan had to offer. Their commitment to the church began to wane as their desire for "free love" grew. The church wasn't reaching them, so para-church organizations began to entice them. A cry went out from the church leadership for caring youth sponsors. Pastors began to see the need for a strong commitment to youth ministry. They realized there really was a generation gap that needed bridging. The answer for most ministries was a youth pastor.

I survived the teen years, left for college and returned to my church to serve as youth pastor. This was a new idea, hiring someone whose duties were devoted and committed only to the youth program. Not only did I plan youth ministry, but I also attempted to build and nurture relationships with the teens and their friends. What an assignment!

Creative Ministry

Here we are again at another opportunity to evaluate the situation and understand the need for change in our ministry to youth. In their book, *High School Ministry,* authors Yaconelli and Burns observed, "In 1986, a general sampling of youth workers by Youth Specialties indicated that 35 to 75 percent of the adolescents in any group are not living with both of their natural families. The stable underpinning of the family is not just buckling—it has collapsed."

Students in our youth groups are often being raised by one parent, or even by no parents. The void left by the lack of caring and concerned parents has forced them to look for support and acceptance in other areas of society. Gangs and peer groups now formulate their belief systems. The search for heroes has turned to the music and media of their day, which are often immoral.

Suicide is the third leading cause of death. According to the Centers for Disease Control, between 1990 and 1996 the teenage suicide rate decreased 13 percent. But between 1962 and 1996, the teenage suicide rate increased 155 percent. Illegal drug use is up among adolescents. According to the Alan Guttmacher Institute, in 1998, almost 1 million teenage girls in the United States get pregnant every year. Fifty-five percent of those pregnancies end in births; 31 percent result in abortions; and 14 percent result in miscarriages. Seventy-eight percent of teenage pregnancies were unplanned. The high schools in many urban areas now have nurseries as a part of their facilities to provide day care for the girls while they finish their secondary education. How can the church respond? In order to minister in these changing times, we must seek God for guidance in making an impact on these lives.

Times have changed! Youth ministry is not even close to what it was when today's church leaders were growing up! The church has lost a generation by portraying God as one who sits on a throne with a gun ready to zap anyone who does wrong. The challenges before us are great! There is a need for mentors to assist the youth pastor and youth leaders in providing Biblical discipleship. Flexible leadership is an prerequisite, because many leaders grew up with different traditions and rules.

To reach today's generation, careful thought must be given to our teaching. Many young people continue to view Christianity as a set of traditions and rules. The inherent need for faith and religion has led some young people to leave their home church and create an individualized faith. They long for peace, understanding and a caring God. However, many were raised in an environment where God was not portrayed as loving and caring. It's time to make certain that our teaching agrees with the Word of God!

Creativity is necessary to compete with MTV, shopping malls, arcades and various other attractions. We must be open to whatever God wants us to do, in His way. Young people need a place to call their own. We must give them ownership and allow them to create their own youth room. It may not look like what we would design, but that's OK.

Music is one of the most important influences in young peoples's lives because it reflects their philosophy of life, their heroes, their lifestyles and their values. One advantage today's youth leader has is the wide variety of Christian music styles that are available. This variety can be an instrument of evangelism. We can offer music by Christian artists who perform a style of music the youth prefer.

Using Today's Technology

In his report, *Third Millennium Teens,* George Barna, found that a majority of teenagers use the

Internet during a typical day. Of the two-thirds who use the Internet, 51 percent participate in on-line discussions or chat rooms. He also notes that one out of every six surveyed said that the Internet would probably be used as a substitute for a traditional church or religious experience within the next five years. That number triples to 46 percent when the time frame is expanded to the next 10 years. Is the church preparing for this type of change? What about a youth church site on the web?

As we endeavor to build a generation of godly young people, we must understand the beliefs of the times. One great concern is in the area of moral truth—knowing right from wrong. In his recent survey, Barna also found the following:

- Seven out of 10 teens say there is no absolute moral truth and eight out of 10 claim that all truth is relative to the individual and his/her circumstances.

- Two out of three teenagers surveyed believe that sometimes you have to break the rules just to get by in life.

- Three-quarters of teens agree that you can tell if something is morally right if it works in your life.

- Eighty percent of those surveyed believe that when it comes to the matter of morals and ethics, truth means different things to different people; no one can be absolutely positive that they know the truth.

Combating Relativism

Our teens are following the path of relativism. Is this because the church has failed to provide teaching and exhortation that is relevant to their needs? Maybe so. If they are not taught absolute truth, there is no need for evangelism. Evangelism without the acceptance of moral absolutes is futile because if there is no right and wrong, there is no sin.

The challenge becomes greater when you look at the priorities of the adults and parents in our congregations. Most of them are more concerned with their bank accounts, pay raises, job promotions, bigger houses and nicer cars than they are about finding the true meaning of life. This has resulted in a generation who does not know God. Many surveys have proven that parents are the greatest influence in their children's lives. Therefore, church leaders must understand that youth ministry in this changing world cannot be a solo act by a youth leader or youth pastor. Rather, the importance of the family and its influence on the child must be considered. When we influence the parents, we can have a greater impact on the child.

Building Relationships

One of the ways we can start building relationships is through the structure of small groups within the overall youth group. Since young prople prize relationships, the opportunity for building those relationships should be provided. Due to some "absentee parents," there is a great need for adult role models. In a day when bigger is often believed to be better, we must consider the need of a personal atmosphere that will foster spiritual growth and discipleship.

Jesus exemplified the small group ministry. This type of ministry can be used to train young people, as well as youth workers. It should begin initially with a small group of prospective small-group leaders. The leader of this initial group should be the youth pastor or youth leader. Leadership principles, discipleship principles and relationship-building skills must be taught and modeled. At the conclusion of this small-group experience, those involved are then permitted to begin other small groups. The leader will guide the young people in their search for identity and healthy relationships. This approach also provides an opportunity for the leader to keep a close eye on each young person's growth.

As mentioned in an earlier chapter, there is great ethnic diversity in most towns and communities. Therefore, careful thought and attention must be given to the activities and programs planned. Racial slurs and comments cannot be permitted. Jokes and stories about people who have different ethnic backgrounds should be left out. In order to teach respect, the leaders must model it in every aspect of ministry. Issues will arise as a result of the various cultures represented in the groups. Each need must be covered in prayer and approached with caution and consideration. Multicultural ministry requires research on the part of the youth leader to know what is and what is not acceptable. Sometimes this information is learned as relationships are built.

Cross-Cultural Ministry

One of the results of the multiethnic ministry is a burden and vision for missions. Summer missions trips, innercity outreach and outreach activities are welcomed by the present generation. They have a strong desire to serve and can be trained for cross-cultural ministry. They are also willing to sacrifice to see lives changed.

Changes in structure must be done with careful thought and prayer. The young people may not be capable of handling sudden and extreme changes. Creative youth leaders should recruit a team to work with them in evaluating each change. The church must understand that it's not the program that makes the difference. Young people are not looking for a new program—there are too many options already competing for their attention. However, if they can develop meaningful relationships, then they can be more effective. Real and honest friendship are high on the priority list of young people. This may mean separating the ministry into junior high ministry, senior high ministry and college/career ministry. Because youth are maturing at a younger age, there may be the need to separate the young teens from the older teens. Their needs and interests are unique and the ministry to them must also be unique.

One of the trends in youth ministry today is the youth church. Teens are flocking to services that are geared to their needs in the following ways:

- The music is their style.
- The atmosphere is casual.
- The praise and worship team and leader are their peers.
- The musicians and greeters are their friends.

There is excitement when young people enter a service that has been planned just for them. They testify of God's work in their lives because they come expecting to experience the presence of God and His supernatural work. Sacrifice is OK with them as long as there are no set expectations and unspoken rules for the order of service. They come longing for something different—something that transcends the hypocritical world in which they live. Even to the point of martyrdom, they choose to believe.

Addressing Violence

Cassie Bernall walked into the school library on the morning of April 20, 1999, to prepare for her English class assignment. Before she could complete her assignment and leave for the next period, two classmates stormed the school. Killing as many people as they could, they confronted her with the question, "Do you believe in God?" She answered, "Yes."

Teen violence is an issue contemporary youth pastors must face. Kentucky, Oregon, Arkansas and Colorado have experienced the violence of teen shootings. The church has an obligation to address this culture that lures kids into destructive behavior.

They must help teens who are struggling emotionally and spiritually by counteracting the negative impact the media has made through television, films, music and games.

Perhaps our hope lies in the attitude and spirit of the young people who have been affected by the violence—young people who . . .

- Are willing to stand in the hallway of their school for a time of prayer, openly professing their faith
- Encounter gunfire and death in the sanctuary the evening following a *See You at the Pole* rally
- Look their killer in the eye and confess their faith in God
- Like the 15 who lost their lives in Timiasora, Romania; because they sang songs of worship in spite of the command to stop. Their acts of faith initiated a revolution that brought freedom of religion to that country.

We have a great responsibility to train the second largest generation of Americans. The number of teenagers in America will grow at twice the rate as the rest of the population during the next decade, peaking in 2080 with approximately 30.8 million teenagers. These teenagers are searching for truth. They need affirmation, encouragement, relationship, honesty and guidance. They have demonstrated an amazing obedience to the call of God and the demands of Scripture. This is evidenced through their participation in ministry and discipleship training, like the Master's Commission. They are choosing to remain sexually pure until marriage, as evidenced by campaigns like *True Love Waits*.

In telling our story to this generation, we must not cloud the issue by expecting them to respond just as we would. They are members of the body of Christ. Let's respect their convictions and pray for them, encouraging them and trusting God to speak to them about the various issues of their daily walk with Him.

I recall the early 70s when the Jesus movement was just beginning. Young people were openly expressing their commitment with a radical faith. There was some rebellion on their part—rebellion against the values of their parents who were self-seeking and achievement oriented. They were seeking for the missing pieces in their lives. They began to find it in Christ.

In the community where my dad was pastoring, a music festival was held. I'm quite sure that everything that went on at that festival was not godly. However, on Sunday morning, some of the young people came to our church. They had slept in their cars in the parking lot and were waiting when we arrived for service. They weren't dressed like us. They were barefoot and their long hair was not clean. When some of the congregation saw these young people, their attitudes reflected disapproval. Instead of being happy that these young people had come to church, they judged and criticized their appearance. I often wonder if that might be our attitude today.

The world around us is changing. A different generation comprises church youth groups, and the next to follow will be different still. Our challenge is to raise a generation of godly leaders to lead the next generation to a knowledge of the unchanging truth of the gospel.

The worst danger that confronts the younger generation is the example set by the older generation.

(Unknown)

Change seldom comes cheap. It has a price tag of time, money, and people.

Leith Anderson, *Dying for Change*

Crossing Generational Ministry

5

Endeavoring to keep the unity of the Spirit in the bond of peace. There is one body and one Spirit.

Ephesians 4:3,4, TM

The news was difficult to grasp. My dad had accepted a new pastorate. The state overseer was meeting with the congregation to elect a new pastor. I watched as the members stood in favor of their preferred pastoral candidate. The vote was split, 50/50. Looking at the sanctuary, the middle aisle was the literal dividing line. Those on the right side voted for the older candidate; those on the left side voted for the younger candidate. I suppose this was the first time the overseer had experienced such a split vote; but it illustrated the make-up of that congregation.

Five Generations of Americans

The church was comprised of older members with traditional ways. My dad had led them in making some changes, but not without serious controversy. For example, when a new addition was planned, the older members thought it wasn't necessary. The dark, dimly-lit basement with its narrow stairway and halls met their needs, or so they thought. When the addition was completed, some did not attend, choosing instead to sit in the cold sanctuary. What a challenge for the next pastor! There were two generations, with a third one on its way, and each had a different ideology and philosophy of ministry.

In his book, *The Second Coming of the Church*, George Barna refers to five generations of Americans listed in the chart below.

Five Generations of Americans

Generation	Years of Birth	Age Range in 1998	Population Size
Seniors	1926 and older	72 and older	19.9 million
Builders	1927-1945	53 to 71	39.8 million
Boomers	1946-1964	34 to 52	73.1 million
Busters	1965-1983	15 to 33	72.2 million
Mosaics	1984-2002	14 and younger	61.7 million*

*Total through 1997

Source: U.S. Bureau of the Census

The Boomer generation focused their beliefs on achievement. No price was too great for them to pay if the reward meant a promotion for them. Boomers still have this philosophy of life today. The Buster generation, followed by the Mosaic generation, rebelled against that notion. Their motivation is toward people, not self-elevation.

For local church leaders the challenge to please everyone has never been greater! Older adults are unwilling to accept new ideas and new technologies. They have experienced the move of God in their lives and see no need for change. The progress of technology and the expansion of information only makes them more leery of leadership. Comfort is more important to them than adapting their ways. If their methods worked before, they will also work now. What they don't realize is that times have changed and they can't expect the same results they had in the "good ole' days." They are glorifying the past and forgetting the hardships they experienced.

The keys to successful ministry in a congregation made up of so many generations are flexibility, bridge building and appreciation for the heritage they have provided. We must acknowledge the traditions and customs that provided constancy and sustenance for them. Radical change will only bring upheaval, division and strife. Change must come slowly, showing appropriate respect to those who paved the way before us.

We in Pentecostal circles would be wise to learn from the Jewish practice of passing faith to the next generation. Granted, we do not want to focus on tradition; however, there is something to be said for the older teaching the younger. We should provide opportunities in our church structure for the younger generations to hear the stories and testimonies of God's provision experienced by former generations. This can be accomplished through dialogue between the generations. It may have to be programmed into our structure, but the benefits of doing so will build bridges between the generations.

Teaching by Example

I remember as a youngster hearing elders in the church share their experiences of salvation and baptism. I recall hearing Sister Richards in Aurora, Illinois, describe her salvation experience and water baptism in the icy water of a creek. Her experience encouraged me. Listening to other elders in church services, as well as during times of fellowship at church dinners, helped me understand their ways. Paul told Titus to share his wisdom. Part of the discipleship process is for the older to teach the younger. In his letter to Titus, Paul lists the qualities of a sound church. One of those qualities is for the older women to provide a proper example and teach the young women (Titus 2:3-5). In order for this to be successful, a relationship of mutual love, care and trust must be built. It becomes the responsibility of the local church leadership to provide an environment where this directive can materialize.

To encompass the broader audience, we must be sensitive to the older age-groups, understanding the limitations of change within their scope of ministry. Then, we must penetrate the culture of the younger groups in a culturally relevant, yet Biblical, manner. One area to be addressed is praise and worship.

Young adults want to experience worship in a relevant way. They want to serve and believe in a God who understands them. They have seen hypocritical members who professed religion, but did not show any evidence of faith in their daily living. The Busters want to discuss their faith. They are looking to the church to help them cope. Open to different views, they accept those who believe differently without judging them. They want a personal encounter with God, but they do not know how to experience it. The emotional experience is not enough—they long for a genuine relationship with God. They are turned off to rituals, religion and organizational structure. Loyalty to one church or denomination is not a priority. Since many of the Busters are single, small groups may help them deal with the issues with which they are struggling.

Ministering to the Boomers

Boomers are returning to church, looking for hope and help. After seeking the "American dream" they find themselves lonely, in debt and with few friends. Climbing the corporate ladder is a priority to them.

They arrive in our churches with all this baggage. We must be aware of their expectations and meet them at their point of need. We can do this in the following ways:

- Organize small groups that deal with relative issues.
- Show professionalism in church programs, structure and procedures.

- Avoid church politics—it is the same thing they live with in the corporate world.
- Emphasize time management.

Pastors and church leaders who are not open to their suggestions and ideas will not welcome their participation. Since family is so important to them, the church must not compete for their family time. These Boomers long for a church that will address the needs of their family members, while not pulling them apart. Their worship must be relevant so that it will minister to their need for fellowship, honesty and integrity. As long as there is opportunity for their input and involvement, they will welcome change that is brought about in a professional way.

Ministering to the Builders

The Builders are predictable. They live in the same house for years, work at the same job until retirement, maintain the same friendships for their entire lives and vacation in the same location every year. They are loyalists who frequent the same places of business for years. Accepting the fact that life is not perfect, they are determined to enjoy the simple things. Change is difficult for them because they have difficulty understanding the younger generations and often resent them for wanting change in the church. They have sacrificed to make the church what it is; the thought of change is a threat. Their style is "back to the basics" of Christianity. They believe the church needs to redefine its ministry and not focus on numbers, buildings, politics and power. They long for the old days when everyone was one big happy family—the days when hymns were revered and the order of service was predictable.

Uniting in Prayer

Adult Christian education is changing! While we understand and recognize these generational differences, the challenge of the local church is to meet their needs with much prayer, wisdom and guidance of the Holy Spirit. God has equipped us with the necessary tools to build the church He desires. In order to do that, we must seek Him fervently. According to Ephesians 6:12, we know that our battle is with spiritual powers. Satan's goal is to keep us divided. He knows that if we are divided, we can be conquered.

Prayer is an area of interest to every age group. We are experiencing the greatest prayer revival in history. When prayer is employed in the right way, more is accomplished for the Lord in a shorter period of time. When people unite in prayer, the Holy Spirit unites them in mind and purpose.

Nebuchadnezzar understood this concept. He knew that if he could unite the people religiously, he could unite them politically. He built a statue of gold and commanded the people to worship it. What he did not understand was that worship cannot be commanded. True worship is a matter of the heart.

As church leaders, we must strive to unite the generations through the medium of prayer. In the seasons of prayer, the Holy Spirit breaks down dividing walls so that God can reveal His will and purpose. One of the greatest hindrances to unity among the generations is the absence of a united purpose and mission. The church will not succeed if its mission has been created and determined by man. Rather, the congregation must seek the face of God by utilizing prayer partners, prayer summits and prayer meetings.

The Church of God in Milford, Ohio, where my dad pastored for more than 10 years, heard him emphasize prayer from the time he accepted the pastorate. For several years, he went to the church on Tuesday evening to conduct a prayer meeting. Often, it was just him and one other couple who attended. Church difficulties kept him on his knees. There was resistance to change from the generations represented among the adult population of the congregation. He kept praying and encouraging others to pray. The Tuesday evening prayer meetings continued.

After nine years, he began to see a breakthrough in the mindset of the congregation. A group of 15 to 20 men, representing all three generational groups, began to meet voluntarily on Sunday mornings at 7:30 for a small group prayer meeting. As God moved in their midst, others began to hunger for prayer. The Tuesday night prayer meeting continued to grow. During that time, division and strife continued in the congregation. However, as the people prayed, a new unity began to prevail. Walls began to crumble. A new spirit of praise and worship was born, resulting in a breakthrough. Both prayer meetings continue today.

In changing times, prayer must increase throughout the church, endeavoring to reach beyond generational lines. In order to be effective, every faction must hear from God—the pastoral staff, the choir director, the ushers and greeters—everyone must pray. As the leadership and staff unite in prayer, they will hear from heaven, and God will heal their hurts and bridge the generational gaps.

Customizing Programs

As we endeavor to reach multiple generations, consideration must also be given to other changes in the church. Many congregations see the need for additional staff in order to minister to various age groups. Often, when pastors in the area retire, they are no longer considered useful, when in reality they can be a great blessing to the local church. They understand the Builder generation and the Senior generation and can give pastoral care and guidance to members of all generations in the local church. Monthly fellowship activities, dinners, luncheons and trips can be geared to their needs. Occasionally, church services can be directed to suit their musical tastes and preaching styles. The wise pastor should take advantage of the experience of a retired minister in the congregation.

Structured small groups can assist in meeting the varied needs of the multiple generations. These groups can be a part of the Sunday school ministry or small groups that focus on the interests of the generations represented.

Accountability is needed for all God's children. When a church ministers to a variety of age groups, many issues can be addressed and accountability can transpire. For the Busters, a small group setting will afford them the privilege of studying and exploring the Scriptures in order to evaluate their faith and relationship with God. It also gives them an avenue to develop much-needed relationships. For the Boomers, small groups provide support for divorcees, single adults, aging parents and many others. Participation in small groups also gives them a place to serve and utilize the gifts God has given them. Small groups can be a less threatening way to witness to non-Christians friends. For the Builders, small groups provide the much-needed fellowship and support. Some churches organize their entire church structure around the concept of small groups. (For more information, refer to *The Cell Church*, by Larry Stockstill.)

As we address the needs of multigenerations, we must evaluate the church structure and its programs to determine if we are alienating any particular group of adults. The following questions will assist in the evaluation:

- Does our praise and worship only minister to a specific group?
- Could we incorporate a greater variety of music so that each generation begins to know and respect the music preference of a different generation?
- Is our program geared to one specific age group?
- Have our Sunday school classes been structured appropriately to reach their respective students?
- Are we providing opportunities for bridge building from one generation to the next?

- Could we benefit by some fellowship opportunities to bring together individuals from various generations?
- Is our leadership style catering to one particular group of people? Are we endeavoring to be led by the Spirit?
- Are we involving individuals from each generation as we make decisions and plans for the future of the church, allowing them to share their stories with each other?
- Are we utilizing the gifts and abilities of individuals from all age groups in the various ministries of the local church?
- Would small-group ministry benefit us in our goal to meet everyone's needs and evangelize individuals of every generation?
- Is there any group we have neglected because we don't understand them? What can we do to reach them?

Nehemiah became a great leader because the people knew he had a heart for them. Nehemiah worked with the people and that made his mission successful. To reach every generation within a local church and community, the key player will be the pastor who cares for them.

And He Himself gave some . . . for the equipping of the saints for the work of ministry, for the edifying of the body of Christ
(Ephesians 4:11,12, *NKJV*).

There is nothing permanent except change.

Heraclitus

Reaching the Changing Generation

6

2 Timothy 1:5, NLT

I know you sincerely trust the Lord, for you have the faith of your mother, Eunice, and your grandmother, Lois.

How should we structure our adult Christian education program? Studies indicate that we are losing the young adults in our church who have no interest in attending Sunday school. They're not like their parents and grandparents. Church isn't a priority in their lives.

What is the answer? I believe they need a megadose of commitment.

I listened intently to a church leader who was

expressing his concerns about this very situation. The church desires to reach all adults, including those who were raised in the church, but who are now sporadic in their attendance. The Millennials, as they have been called, appear to be unconcerned and indifferent to local church ministry.

This younger adult generation lives for now. Nothing shocks them. Change for them is constant. They take consumerism for granted because they have had everything handed to them and they don't trust older adults.

Many churches do not understand the differences in the generational groups present in their congregations and described in the chart in chapter 5. Some sociologists divide the adult population into as many as five unique groups.

The waves of change grow stronger with each generation, because they are connected to each other with common boundaries and common characteristics. These characteristics identify the changes the church must address to impact each generation. Most churches do not have the luxury of working with only one generation. Since all generations are present, our ministry to adults must be all-inclusive.

Different generations are looking for different characteristics in their search for a meaningful religious experience. The challenge of local church leaders is to bridge the gap between the adults by ministering to the unique needs of each. Today the Boomers, who left the church for years because they considered it irrelevant to their lives, are returning.

They need help relating to and understanding their children. They want a contemporary style of worship with a relative message. Their agenda includes specialized ministries to help them with their daily tasks. On the other hand, the Builders and Seniors generations want to hold on to the truth as they see it. After all, it has stood the test of time. Why change now? The Busters are searching for meaning, integrity, relationship and experience. They don't care about format or traditions. Change is great because nothing is constant in their lives.

As we consider the differences that created the generational groups, we must understand that the Word of God remains constant. It is pertinent and relative to every individual. In Christian education, our goal is to see lives changed. If we do not see lives changed as the result of our teaching and training, we are wasting our time and effort. In order to understand the change, it will be helpful to look at an overview of each adult generation, along with various options for reaching them.

Reaching the Millennial Generation

Young adults, the Millennials, have a variety of needs. They long for intimacy with friends and family. As they become independent in their lifestyle, they begin the process of breaking ties with the past, including the church. How can the church respond to this changing group?

We can . . .

- Give them a place to belong.

- Accept their singleness. Many of them are choosing to remain single longer, some for life.
- Involve them in congregational life.
- Provide ministries that meet their needs. For example, they may see quality nursery care and clean nursery facilities as a determining factor in their search!
- Offer small-group ministry, that provides a format for building intimacy.
- Integrate intergenerational learning opportunities that will provide opportunities to learn from others.

Reaching the Buster Generation

The generation of Busters represent the second largest group of young adults in U.S. history. Their parents have had dual-careers. Demographers tell us they have created their own culture. It is no wonder that many have classified them as Generation X because they have no identity of their own. They are a group of individuals who have little in common with each other. Many of them have no spiritual identity and the church seems unsure of how to help them. Their theme song appears to be "I Gotta Be Me." They are dreamers who need direction for God's will in their lives. They change careers often and without a great amount of thought.

How can the church respond? The church can . . .

- Define its vision. They want to know where the ministry is headed.
- Offer classes on Biblical parenting.
- Teach and demonstrate unconditional love.
- Provide Christian daycare.
- Update the worship service, including a blending of the traditional and contemporary, particularly in the music.
- Provide service opportunities for this generation to understand the necessity of giving and not just receiving.
- Provide fellowship opportunities, using small groups. This is a generation characterized by aloneness.
- Offer relative and up-to-date learning opportunities that relate to their daily living.

Reaching the Boomers

With this generation of adults, loyalty is a thing of the past. Because of so many options available, they will choose what is most meaningful to them. For the most part, they have dropped out of church and turned away from the faith of their parents. Some are returning, finding new levels of commitment. They watched their parents struggle financially. Their experiences were limited growing up. However, they want their children to experience a different lifestyle and they are doing everything within their power to help them do so. How can the church respond to this changing generation?

- By providing strong urban churches. Boomers like the cities. Churches who minister to the Boomers will strive for effective urban ministry.
- By considering the names and titles in our ministries. The Boomers don't like rigid labels. Even the name of our ministry may influence their involvement.
- By helping them discover their calling and then equipping them to carry out that calling. They want to be trained for ministry!
- By giving them space as their job responsibilities continue to grow. This may require careful thought and consideration because of the length of time and commitment required of the workers and teachers.
- By providing an effective youth ministry.
- By offering short-term missions involvement opportunities.
- By giving them options for ministry involvement.
- By streamlining the ministry structure.
- By using visual aids wherever and whenever possible.
- By emphasizing celebration in worship, restructuring the worship service where possible.
- By emphasizing the family.

Reaching the Builders and Seniors

Builders and Seniors generations alike resist change. They believe the way they and their parents did things is the best way. They were born before the invention of television, Frisbees, computers, ballpoint pens and CDs. They were raised in a society that didn't give them many choices, so they survived by remaining loyal. They "buy American." They are hard workers and big savers. Having fought in at least one war, they are usually patriotic. They want to know people, but have great concern about sharing their hurts and needs too deeply. Displays of affection are often taboo for them. It is difficult for them to tolerate people who are different. Adversity provides them the opportunity to stick together and work hard. They grew up attending Sunday school and continue with this habit. The church can consider the following options:

- Emphasize Sunday school.
- Offer missions involvement opportunities.
- Provide in-depth Bible study.
- Focus on marriage and grandparenting.
- Prioritize pastoral care.
- Provide group activities.

Evaluation

As we address the needs of the generations, attention must be given to specific needs of each group. This will require evaluating our church structure and its programs to determine if we are alienating any particular group of adults. Church leaders must address the following questions:

- Does our praise and worship only minister to a specific group?
- Could we incorporate a greater variety of music, so that each generation begins to know and respect the music preference of a different generation?
- Is our program geared to one specific age group?
- What about our Sunday school organization? Have our classes been structured appropriately? Have the teachers been trained to teach in a manner that will reach their respective class of students?
- Are we providing opportunities for "bridge building" from one generation to the next?
- Could we benefit by offering more fellowship opportunities to bring together individuals from various generations?
- Is our leadership style catering to one particular group of people? Or are we endeavoring to be led by the Spirit?
- Are we so determined to change the mind-set that we have become insensitive to people's needs and preferences?

- Are we involving individuals from each of the generations as we make decisions and plans for the future of the church?
- Are we giving opportunities for the older generations to pass their faith along by telling their story? And are we giving opportunities for the younger believers to share their story with the older believers?
- Are we utilizing the gifts and abilities of individuals of all age groups in the various ministries of the church?
- Would small-group ministry benefit us in our goal of meeting everyone's needs, as well as evangelism of individuals of every generation?
- Is there any group we have pushed aside because we don't understand them? What can we do to reach them?

Technology's Impact on Adults

Adults are confronted with all sorts of vices challenging their faith. Technology has influenced our educational efforts. How can we as a church address the impact of technology? Furthermore, how can we utilize technology in our ministries? Are we taking advantage of the instruments that characterize the generation we are trying to reach? For example, should we include the use of certain programs on television in our classes? Using the material from these programs as a catalyst for critical thinking could enhance the learning process and at the same time give the students an opportunity to evaluate their viewing practices. What about a study of violence on television?

Have our values been affected by the Internet? Has advertising caused an undercurrent that is eroding our culture and eventually our values? The older adults have grown up with television, while the younger adults need to be challenged with the changes that have occurred. This can be accomplished through careful study in a group of adults with representatives from each generational group. Perhaps Paul understood this principle when he talked about the influence Timothy's mother and grandmother had on Timothy's life. There must be time for interaction between the age groups!

The Role of Special Interests

Special interests continue to captivate the attention of the adult population. In order to make an impact on all the generations in our congregations, we must consider a variety of learning experiences.

People have never been busier than they are today. They have less free time than ever before even though they have access to more information through technological advances. Our approach to ministry must have a servant mentality that involves the church as a vessel to minister to the needs of the individual. This will include small-group ministry, practical elective study opportunities, support groups—anything that reaches out to meet the needs of the church, as well as those we are trying to reach outside our congregation.

Time for a Change

The traditional approach to Christian education includes an adult Sunday school class that meets in the sanctuary each Sunday morning. This will not suffice for the varied needs in the different generations. These adults are searching for truth. They must be given opportunities for interaction and fellowship in a nonthreatening environment. They are struggling with keeping their families and their marriages intact. Financial problems are a great concern. Many are even questioning their faith. They long for relevant teaching and preaching as they become independent of their parents and teachers. This creates a need for guidance to help them develop their faith and value system.

The church must be careful not to segregate their learning experiences from their daily living. This means the church cannot afford to create classes and ministries just to keep the congregational machinery operating. Rather, the goal of adult ministry should be to prepare and equip adults for effective living, as they strive to realize their God-given potential. Where do they fit in God's plan? How can God's plan work after their life has fallen apart?

It is true that some churches have begun targeting specific population groups. Some focus on Boomers, while others go after the Busters. However, for most traditional churches, this kind of focus is not possible because they have representatives from each generation.

Bridging the Gap

The area where a blending of the generations can occur in ministry is in the worship service. Other ministries can focus on the needs of the various groups of adults. Varying the style of worship will appeal to different groups of people. If hymns have been the order of the day in each service, then hymns should be incorporated in the change. If the piano has been the primary instrument, then effective change does not simply eliminate it in order to create a different style of music. Changing the style of worship to minister to all age groups can be tricky. Each change must be bathed in prayer and well planned. The following steps may serve as a helpful guide:

Step 1. Secure the support of the pastor. Without the pastor's endorsement, change cannot happen!

Step 2. Recruit lay leaders in the planning in order to gain their support.

Step 3. Introduce the vision to the congregation. Help them see what can be accomplished as the result of the proposed change.

Step 4. Emphasize in classes, small groups and preaching, how God created us as unique individuals with diverse opinions.

Step 5. Give the change a trial run through a second worship service or alternative meetings.

Step 6. Help the different generations understand each other by educating them in the characteristics of each group in a noncritical manner. Provide a forum for discussing the unique values and strengths of each generation.

Step 7. Program opportunities for the members of the different generations to mix and mingle their ideas.

Step 8. Provide opportunities for members of all age groups to be involved in the leadership of the local church.

Who is visible on the platform? Is only one age group represented on the worship team? If so, it will primarily influence that particular group. Make the praise and worship team intergenerational. What about the ministry staff? Are all generational groups represented?

Nothing stays the same. Generations are changing. The Builders are growing older, ministry styles are dissipating. For the sake of the future of the church, we must educate the Boomers about financial stewardship. The Boomers will respond to people, projects and vision. Because of their loyalty to personal relationships, they'll accept an invitation to lunch, but will turn down an invitation to a men's breakfast. Only simple structure programs built around people will survive under Boomers' leadership. Ministries that do not make a difference in people's lives will dissolve.

As Busters rise to leadership, they will call the church back to traditional values, such as family. If they believe in a cause, they will support it with their time and finances. Their internal needs will be great because they are the most hurting generation to come our way in some time. Since their interests are tied close to the home, the church will be encouraged to look at ministry in their own area, rather than ministering around the world.

Effective Change Agents

Yes, change will come with each new generation of adults. We will start new ministries. We'll find ourselves modifying older ministries and programs. We will probably be forced to eradicate programs that were successful in the past but have no validity in the present. It won't be easy.

As we look to the future and prepare to bridge the generation gaps in our ministries, we cannot ignore the past. In fact, it would be wise to bless the past and those who have paved the road before us and set the tone for the present.

In making changes in adult ministries, leadership must show respect for all. This will mean affirming what worked in the past without criticizing the present. This affirmation will show respect for those who were involved in those programs. Then changes can be based on Biblical principles that underlie both the previous methods and the proposed changes. By building on the past, you can integrate a new integrate a new approach. In urban and suburban areas of the United States, it normally takes five to seven years to turn an existing church in a new direction. If the church is located in a rural area, it may take as long as 12 years to see change. Effective change takes time and patience.

Lord, You have been our dwelling place in all generations
(Psalm 90:1, *NKJV*).

In this era of rapid and profound change, we know that the shape of the church must change significantly if it is to remain both alive and influential. The likely structural changes that will redefine the church must be taken seriously. We must be prepared to reengineer the contours of ministry without compromising its content.

George Barna, *The Second Coming of the Church*

Shifting Sunday School

7

W.A. Criswell

From God's own hand, Sunday school is a gift from heaven.

I have often started workshops and conferences with this quote by W.A. Criswell, the great Baptist minister. The looks I receive after making this statement, along with silence that follows, is evidence that most people no longer believe this way. Pastors are struggling to keep their congregations interested in Sunday school. Sunday school superintendents and Christian education directors have difficulty recruiting workers and teachers because members no longer see the need. Some have discarded the concept of Sunday school, endorsing extended children's church during morning worship service. Others provide a minimal structure for those still hanging on to their commitment to Sunday school. Still others are gasping for air as they struggle to survive. Is there a future for Sunday school?

Historical Review

The church is in a real dilemma. Historically, we see Sunday school as one of the major evangelistic arms of the local church. Robert Raikes saw the need for educating street children in England. In 1780, he believed he could prevent some major problems by educating the children. So, he took them in, loved them and gave them the opportunity to learn. He harnessed their energy into productive activities. From his initial program of showing compassion, the Sunday school movement was born.

Over the years, we have seen some changes in the strategy for Sunday school. In its initial stages, Sunday school focused on children and teenagers. In the late 1880s, the adults became involved as adult education classes were initiated. Then, Sunday school began to grow and attendance escalated through the 1950s. Everyone was attending Sunday school—it was a priority in the home. Families understood the importance of Christian education through Sunday school. Sunday school attendance surpassed the worship attendance and became the primary entry point for new people to enter the church.

In the 1960s, the emphasis in Sunday school began

to turn from evangelism and outreach to spiritual growth and nurture. This inward focus stifled the growth spurt Sunday school had enjoyed. As the ministry staff in the local church increased, the responsibility for evangelism was funneled in their direction. In turn, the laity saw their role as that of building disciples, while evangelistic rallies and revivals emphasized evangelism. Churches began to utilize buses, and due to large bus ministries, the attendance in many churches began to improve and Sunday school saw some increase. However, as the emphases on spiritual growth within continued, the outreach lessened and attendance declined again. As a result, maintenance became the order of the day.

Goals of Sunday School

As we evaluate possible reasons Sunday school has declined, we must answer the following questions: First of all, what is the purpose of the Sunday school? Are we still conducting Sunday school for the sake of tradition? In this paradigm shift, should we not stop and evaluate the whole process?

Evangelism continues to be a strong goal of Sunday school ministry. Class members bring friends to hear the Word of God, which makes Sunday school a viable entry point into the church. However, if seekers are encouraged to attend these small-group Bible studies, careful thought and attention must be given by the teacher, facilitator or small-group leader. To prohibit further decline, every church needs to develop a purpose statement for their Sunday school that includes a vision statement.

This should be followed by a mission statement that spells out a step-by-step process to fulfill the vision. The vision must be a God-given vision, not a man-made idea.

Reasons for Decline

I am convinced that God has different purposes for different Sunday schools in different communities. The thousands of children who are picked up weekly in New York City by Metro Ministries are ministered to because of the evangelistic vision of Pastor Bill Wilson. The children taught each Sunday morning at the North Cleveland Church of God in Cleveland, Tennessee, are the recipients of a different vision and mission thrust. Too often, church leadership has been guilty of transplanting the vision and mission of one church or ministry into another church that has different needs. God has a unique purpose for every ministry. Our goal should be to listen to His voice so that we can see the vision He has for us. Once the vision and mission statement is developed, plans can proceed to fulfill that vision during the coming year.

A second reason for the decline of Sunday school is that it has become too academic. The classroom is arranged with pews, chairs and tables all facing the same direction. In the front of the room is a lectern where the teacher teaches by lectures. There is little opportunity for fellowship and sharing. In order to create an atmosphere of caring and concern, the Sunday school teachers must create a friendly environment.

A third reason for the decline of the Sunday school is attributed to the poor quality of instruction. At one time, public school teachers and Sunday school teachers had similar credentials and expectations. However, the expectations and requirements of secular teachers have risen, while the expectations and requirements of Sunday school teachers have decreased. More teaching materials and resources are available than ever before, but they are not being utilized. Less preparation on the part of the teachers and lack of variety in teaching methods create boredom. We use the top-of-the-line technological equipment on our jobs daily, but when in Sunday school, no technology is being utilized. The excellence they desire and expect is not there.

In addition to not having variety in methodology, the facilities are poor and unkempt and professionalism is lacking. It is evident that the Sunday school ministry is not a priority of the church. Training and evaluation of the facilities, teaching aids and teaching methods must be up-to-date if we value the teaching ministry. If there is no accountability, there will be no progress and lives will not be changed.

Of course, there are always exceptions. I recall one of my favorite teachers in junior high school. She didn't have access to a lot of technology. In fact, our church didn't even own a copy machine. So, she wrote everything out by hand so we could each have our own outline. However, the ingredients that made her class successful included love, creativity, relationship and accountability. She expected us to prepare for each week's lesson. Even though she didn't have many teaching aids, she was creative with what she had. I remember a lesson she taught using popcorn as an illustration. We went to her house and enjoyed the popcorn as she discussed the problem of being puffed up and full of air, without substance. She had a tremendous knowledge of the Word of God. Her example, along with a demonstration of love in a caring environment, created a positive teaching experience for the students.

The fourth reason for the demise of the Sunday school has been the lack of emphasis on Bible study that relates to everyday living. Today, people want the opportunity to discover Bible truths themselves, rather than taking a spectator's approach in the learning process. As a result, we are losing adults in Sunday school. Many of them are dropping their kids off for their classes, then going for breakfast during the Sunday school hour. Boomers want the opportunity to be involved in discussion and interaction!

The Sunday school schedule is something else to consider. Some churches have abandoned their Sunday school program completely. Others have replaced the traditional Sunday school structure with electives offered at various times. Still others are electing to conduct their Sunday school program on Sunday evening, Saturday afternoon, or other times and days of the week. Since people are involved in so many things, it would be wise to determine the time slot that best serves the church's mission.

Sunday school is no longer "child based." In a changing culture where demographics are changing, this ministry has merit for every generation. The church must plan for change by adding classes and Bible studies that minister to the varying needs of the adults. With the emphasis on the family today, some churches are seeing a genuine shift in family involvement in the Christian education process. Parents are the primary Christian educators in the church. The family was instituted by God to build faith and model that faith by passing it from one generation to the next. The church should provide a structure whereby this could be accomplished.

One such structure includes multigenerational classes in small-group settings. In these groups, parents and children meet together to study the Scriptures. The church's role is to equip parents to facilitate the discussion. A multigeneration Sunday school class could meet weekly as an option for those families desiring to fulfill this responsibility through the church structure. The old paradigm of Christian education saw the role of the home supporting the church. The new paradigm is just the opposite—the church supporting the home. If indeed parents have the greatest influence in a child's life, then it makes sense that a primary ministry of the church should be to adequately train and equip the parents to minister to each child.

In his book, *Absolute Confusion*, George Barna supports this need. A 1997 study of American teenagers discovered that "kids who feel connected to their parents or school were less likely to suffer emotional distress, think about suicide, be violent, smoke cigarettes, drink alcohol or smoke marijuana." These parent-nurtured kids also delayed their first sexual experiences. Sunday school needs to become a family affair!

As we evaluate the purpose of Sunday school by today's standards, six tasks surface. Each of these tasks define the role of Sunday school in the local church. Some churches may emphasize one over another, but each task should be represented in the mission statement.

Six Ingredients of Sunday School

1. Evangelism of unbelievers
2. Systematic Bible study
3. Effective teaching and Bible exploration
4. Fellowship
5. Care and unconditional love
6. Leading people to worship God as they get to know Him through the study of His Word

Using these six ingredients, the local church can create a mission statement for Sunday school. The seven stages of vision planning identified by Talmadge Johnson and Stan Toler in their book, *Rediscovering the Sunday School*, is also helpful in gaining a new vision for Sunday school.

1. Praying—relying on the resources God makes available to you

2. Understanding—looking at the emerging trends in today's society
3. Searching—asking, "Why do we have Sunday school?" (focusing on community needs)
4. Defining—asking, "What do we want to accomplish?" (defining the tasks to be accomplished)
5. Identifying—asking, "What is our common goal?" (teach for edification and decision)
6. Processing—asking, "Is our Sunday school ministry effective?"
7. Reforming—making adjustments (keeping the vision current, checking the vital signs)

Evaluation will assist the church leaders in staying on track with their ministry efforts. Goal setting is a vital part of the planning process. There should be goals set for each level of the Sunday school ministry—attendance goals, offering goals and visitation goals. Teachers should be encouraged to set their own goals, preferably with the assistance of the class so that they can have ownership. Acknowledging those who have met their goals—weekly, monthly, quarterly and annually—is a good motivator.

Discovering Spiritual Gifts

Teacher recruitment is a major difficulty facing many churches. One of the primary responsibilities of the local church is to assist the members of the congregation in finding their spiritual gifts and then showing them where and how they can use those gifts. Too often, recruitment is seen as a slot that needs to be filled. We need to change that view by finding a place for every individual to serve. Many churches begin classes and ministries before they find individuals who have a burden and vision for ministry. Consequently, they overwork the faithful. Let's turn the table by assisting members in discovering gifts before we initiate the ministry. We can help prevent burnout of teachers and workers by providing team teachers, shorter time commitments and better training. Monthly motivational meetings will also generate excitement and inspiration.

An annual day of appreciation is another way to express gratitude to teachers for a job well done. Recognizing them and giving them a gift or certificate in front of their peers and students will encourage them. Frequent favors showing thanks will also be well received. Time off for a vacation or birthday, or some other special event, should be granted without making them feel guilty. A weekly efficiency check list can assist in a "Teacher of the Month" program. After the points are tallied monthly, the teacher with the most points is given a special gift, perhaps a gift certificate to a restaurant or Christian bookstore. When planning a worker's appreciation event, don't ask the workers to provide the food. That really takes away the treat.

The practice of exploring spiritual gifts before recruiting teachers will give greater attention to the person, rather than the position. We are in the "people business," not the "position business." It's all about helping people find their places and as a result, experiencing fulfillment. There is no greater organization than the Sunday school for involving members who feel misplaced.

Changing Models

In order to revitalize Sunday school in these changing times, careful thought must be given to changing models. Some things never change—the Word of God for instance. Other things must change. If we look at the history of Sunday school, we find that Sunday school is changeable. It is not sacred. Tradition is not a valid reason for maintaining the model we follow. We must examine the needs of our present-day society and structure a Sunday school that will be truly effective.

The space/facility problem in many churches can be dealt with by offering innovative options. Classes can be held in off-campus locations—restaurants, community centers, sidewalks or members' homes.

Today's adults want choices. Offering electives enables the church to minister to the needs of the congregation, as well as the potential attendee. Elective studies also encourage the formation of new relationships within the church. The "18-month rule" of church growth states that classes or groups that have been meeting for 18 months or longer will seldom be open to newcomers. Providing elective classes and small-group studies will attract visitors and newcomers.

Many Christian adults are illiterate when it comes to a systematic Bible study. They have only participated in topical studies and as a result have not gained the Biblical knowledge that is needed. Elective studies should be screened by the Christian education director, pastor or someone they designate. This will help prevent teaching that is not doctrinally sound. The use of standardized denominational Sunday school curriculum will provide a well-balanced systematic Bible study. Remember, the curriculum is a tool—a means to an end—not the end result.

Sunday school is not just another program we attach to an already overcrowded church schedule—it is a vital arm of the church doing its work of reaching, teaching, winning, training and sending out. It's time for evaluation! The following material will assist in assessing your Sunday school needs.

And everyday, in the Temple and in their homes, they continued to teach and preach this message: "The Messiah you are looking for is Jesus"
(Acts 5:42, *NLT*).

Changes to Consider in Sunday School Ministry:

1. Change the name and the time to Sunday evening or Saturday.
2. Utilize team teachers in classes.
3. Add a bus or van for outreach.
4. Emphasize relationships in small-group ministry.
5. Begin multiple Sunday school sessions.
6. Begin a branch Sunday school, with the purpose of planting a new church.
7. Create Sunday school classes or small groups to meet needs not being met in the community.
8. Organize adult Bible fellowship groups that serve as Sunday school classes.
9. Reduce the commitment required for Sunday school teachers (i.e., six months instead of one year).
10. Conduct surveys to determine why attendance in Sunday school is down. What are their interests?

Recruiting Principles in the 21st Century

1. Ask God to bring those who will serve (Matthew 9:37, 38).
2. Design a winning team that will succeed.

3. Consider the busy schedule of prospective leaders.
4. Avoid long-term commitments.
5. Provide opportunity for advancement.
6. Furnish clear boundaries and directions.
7. Provide written job descriptions; develop and highlight a clear recruitment process.

Practical Application

1. Prayerfully examine your own walk with the Lord.
2. Examine your organization and sell the cause, not the need!
3. Highlight the teaching staff through videos, testimonials, announcements, introductions, special days, and so forth.
4. Develop team-teaching and teacher rotations. Provide classroom aides to do the busy work.
5. Develop a master teacher/apprentice program.
6. Develop a quality teacher-training program.

Five Keys for the Effective Sunday School Class in Changing Times

1. Centered in God (prayer)
2. Caring enough to give every student a job to do

3. Connecting in fellowship
4. Committed to follow-up (within 24 hours of an absence)
5. Communicating on a regular basis via weekly newsletter (written or e-mail)

7 Characteristics of the Shepherd/Teacher

1. LISTEN . . . listens intently for unusual noise that might reflect hidden danger as well as signs of distress from the sheep in trouble.
2. COMMIT . . . to the task assigned; willing to follow through to completion.
3. PROVIDE . . . care and protection so that the sheep will grow as intended.
4. GUIDE . . . shows direction; not a dictator of the route to take, but a guide with a map outlining which way to God; a leader.
5. PROTECT . . . guards the flock, watching for anything that might endanger them; willing to lay down his life to save the sheep.
6. DISCIPLINE . . . "Break the leg" of a wayward sheep to make it dependent upon the shepherd; then in turn lovingly nurse it back to health.
7. FAITHFULLY SERVE . . . all that has been entrusted to your care.

Top Ten Indicators of a Healthy Sunday School

1. *Systematic Bible Study* (2 Timothy 2:15)—involves every age group of the local church in systematic Bible study
2. *Spiritual Formation* (Ephesians 4:14)—builds and nurtures the body
3. *Outreach/Evangelism* (Matthew 28:19, 20)—equips for works of service and soulwinning
4. *Leadership Training* (2 Timothy 2:2)—provides ongoing training for teachers and leaders
5. *Member Involvement* (Acts 2:44-47)—fosters opportunity for relationship building and fellowship
6. *Learning Environment* (Matthew 13)—facilitates a God-centered setting for the teaching-learning experience
7. *Teaching Aids and Resources* (2 Timothy 3:16, 17)—utilizes relevant curriculum supported with appropriate teaching aids and resources
8. *Family Ministry* (Deuteronomy 5; 6)—strengthens marriages, equips parents, enriches family life
9. *Assimilation/Follow-Up* (Ephesians 4:16)—extends care to prospects and integrates them into the church family
10. *Structured for Growth* (John 15:8)—reproduces itself through new classes and new churches

5 Keys for Growth in the Purpose-driven Sunday School Class

1. Centered in God (prayer)
2. Caring enough to involve students. Give everybody a job to do.
3. Connecting in fellowship
4. Communicating on a regular basis (weekly newsletter). "They don't care how much you know until they know how much you care."
5. Committed to follow-up

Memorable Quotes

"If the Lord doesn't bring them, you don't want them!"

"The contentment of your current teachers is your greatest recruitment tool."

"The overall education program should sell itself without any glitter."

"The health of the sheep depends on the heart of the shepherd."

Efficiency Checklist for Sunday School Teachers

Date: ________ Name: ____________________

____ Present (10 points)

____ Prepared lesson (10 points for each hour)

____ Offering (5 points)

____ Bible (5 points)

____ Morning worship (10 points)

____ If you received a second offering in Sunday school class (5 points)

____ If you attended last Wednesday evening service (15 points)

____ If you attended every night of revival last week (25 points)

____ If you attended prayer meeting before class (15 points)

____ If you spent time alone with the Lord every day last week (15 points)

____ For reaching your class goals —10 points for each (20 points)

____ Attendance building method in your class (10 points). Explain:

____

____

____ For each card or call to an absent student. He/she must be contacted to receive the points (5 points)!

____ For each visit to the home of an absentee student (15 points)

____ Were all visitors in your class contacted? (10 points)

____ Did you turn in your follow-up sheet today for last Sunday (25 points)?

___ Did you have a class activity outside of Sunday school during the past six weeks (10 points)?

____ For each visitor in your class today (must be first-time!; 5 points)

____ Did you straighten up your room after using it (10 points)?

____ Have you read the latest AIM/CTC book (10 points)?

____ For each visit to the home of a student whose card has been removed (20 points)

____ Did you use a new teaching method or teaching aid today (10 points)?

_____ **Previous total points**

_____ **Total points today**

_____ **Total points so far this month/this quarter**

There is nothing more difficult to take in hand, more perilous to conduct, or more uncertain in its success, than to take the lead in the introduction of a new order of things.

Niccolo Machiavelli, *The Prince*

Leading the Team

8

Put into practice what you learned from me, what you heard and saw and realized. Do that, and God, who makes everything work together, will work you into his most excellent harmonies.

Philippians 4:9, TM

Changing times require transformational leaders. In order to facilitate change in any ministry, leaders must build a team that will help influence the changes needed. Mike Ditka created the following acronym:

T—Together
E—Everyone
A—Achieves
M—More

This summarizes the goals and purposes of the leadership team. Implementing change in any ministry requires a cooperative effort from the leaders. This prevents the feeling of loneliness at the top—those times when leaders feel like they are the only ones trying to accomplish the task.

The present age is ripe for the team-building style of leadership. The postmodern world wants to know the heart of leadership and see the gospel being lived out in the community of the local church. They will know we are Christian by our love (see John 13:35). The ministry team should build harmony around a common vision of philosophy—not personality or spiritual gifts. Sharing the leadership as a team can greatly enhance the productivity of the ministry.

I once heard the story of a leader who was weary from working so much. He sat down with a pencil and calculator to figure all the time he was spending on the job. His analysis was this:

> Recently, I sat down and asked myself, "Why am I so tired from all the work I do?" After much analysis, I now understand it.
>
> The population of this country is a little over 220 million. Eighty-four million people are over 68 years of age, which leaves 136 million to do the work. People under 20 years of age total 95 million, which leaves only 41 million to do the work.
>
> There are 22 million people employed by the government, which leaves 19 million to do

> the work. Four million are in the Armed Forces, which leaves 15 million to do the work. Deduct 14,800,000 for those people who are in state and city offices, and that leaves only 200,000 to do the work. There are 188,000 in hospitals and insane asylums, so that leaves 12,000 people to do the work.
>
> It may interest you to know that there are 11,998 people in jail, so that leaves just two people to carry the load. That's you and me, brother, and I'm getting tired of doing everything myself.
>
> —Source unknown

There is no substitute for having the right people working with you. They will make or break your ministry leadership team.

Developing Leaders

In this changing world, people need to be trained, empowered and released to fulfill their God-given potential. Too many leaders are sitting at the top crying about loneliness, when it is God's plan for them to develop leaders to surround them. Christ illustrated this principle. When He began His ministry, He called people to walk alongside Him. He saw beyond their natural and human circumstances. He detected their potential and began His mission of discipleship so that they could realize their potential.

The day of solo leadership is past. In order to meet the changing needs of the generations, a leadership team must be in place. Every leader needs people who support them and help them succeed. There are no "Lone Rangers" in the body of Christ. We need each other. A leader who recognizes the uniqueness of each member of the body and identifies their gifts will be successful.

In his book, *Hot Illustrations for Youth Talks,* Wayne Rice shares the story of a man's response to an insurance company that requested information following the initial claim. His response is the following letter:

> Dear Sirs:
>
> I am writing in response to your request concerning clarification of the information I supplied in block #11 on the insurance form, which asked for the cause of the injury. I answered, "Trying to do the job alone." I trust that the following explanation will be sufficient.
>
> I am a bricklayer by trade. On the date of the injury, I was working alone, laying brick around the top of a three-story building. When I finished the job, I had about 500 pounds of brick left over. Rather than carry the bricks down by hand, I decided to put them into a barrel and lower them by a pulley that was fastened to the top of the building.
>
> I secured the end of the rope at ground level, went back up to the top of the building, loaded the bricks into the barrel, and pushed it over the side. I then went back down to the ground and untied the rope, holding it securely to insure

the slow descent of the barrel. As you will note in block #6 of the insurance form, I weigh 145 pounds. At the shock of being jerked off the ground so swiftly by the 500 pounds of bricks in the barrel, I lost my presence of mind and forgot to let go of the rope.

Between the second and third floors I met the barrel. This accounts for the bruises and lacerations on my upper body. Fortunately, I retained enough presence of mind to maintain my tight hold on the rope and proceeded rapidly up the side of the building, not stopping until my right hand was jammed in the pulley. This accounts for my broken thumb (see block #4). Despite the pain, I continued to hold tightly to the rope. Unfortunately, at approximately the same time, the barrel hit the ground and the bottom fell out of the barrel. Devoid of the weight of the bricks, the barrel now weighed about 50 pounds. I again refer you to block #6, where my weight is listed. I began a rapid descent.

In the vicinity of the second floor, I met the barrel coming up. This explains the injury to my legs and lower body. Slowed only slightly, I continued my descent, landing on the pile of bricks. Fortunately, my back was only sprained. I am sorry to report, however, that at this point I again lost my presence of mind and let go of the rope.

I trust this answers your concern. Please note that I am finished trying to do the job alone.[1]

The Bible is filled with examples of team ministry and leadership. Nehemiah's strategy for building the wall of Jerusalem included team work. A ministry team can be defined as a small group of people committed to a specific and unique ministry that enhances and helps to fulfill the mission and purpose of the church.

When individuals understand the power of team leadership, they will utilize the concept that in turn will revitalize their philosophy of leadership. Finding the leaders for the team can be a tremendous challenge. However, be reminded that God has not called you to a ministry that He has not already provided the vision and resources to fulfill that ministry. Christ demonstrated this Biblical model. In the Book of Mark, He appointed 12 apostles, that they might be with Him and that He might send them out (3:14). Paul the apostle believed in teamwork. When he went on missionary journeys, he enlisted the help of Barnabas, Luke, Timothy and Silas. The Book of Ecclesiastes tells us that two are better than one, because they have a good return for their work.

> Two people can accomplish more than twice as much as one; they get a better return for their labor. If one person falls, the other can reach out and help. But people who are alone when they fall are in real trouble. And on a cold night, two under the same blanket can gain warmth from each other. But how can one be warm alone? A person standing alone can be attacked and defeated, but two can stand back-to-back and conquer. Three are

> even better, for a triple-braided cord is not easily broken (Ecclesiastes 4:9-12, *NLT*).

A good team will accomplish more together than individual members could ever accomplish alone. Perhaps this is the reason Paul refers to the members of the body of Christ as having different functions, but one common purpose. The effective leadership team has one purpose and one common goal. As they communicate, they move toward that common goal and an effective team is formed.

Too many churches are being true to the 20/80 principle. This principle is defined as 20 percent of the people in a congregation doing 80 percent of the ministry. Team members need to be involved in all aspects of the local church ministry. Often we operate like a football team in a stadium full of spectators. As Bud Wilkinson, former head football coach at the University of Oklahoma once said, "I define football as 22 men on the field who desperately need rest and 50,000 people in the stands who desperately need exercise." Many leaders in our churches need rest—they are "burned out." Many members on the sidelines desperately need to get involved.

Utilizing the Gifts

The problem with some churches is that they have not learned how to effectively equip their laity for ministry. A spiritual gifts inventory will determine interests, talents, abilities and gifts of the members. Then, ministry can be formulated, utilizing the gifts that are available. This will require an ongoing recruitment program of encouragement and motivation. It is my understanding that an elephant is trained from birth that it does not have the power to remove the stake to which it is tied. Even after maturity, elephants are not tempted to pull out the stake, although they certainly have the strength to do so. They are not realizing their potential because training has disabled them. It is the task of church leaders today to help Christians realize their potential. This can't be done by one man. In order to lead the congregation forward, an effective team builds on the strength of individual members.

Experts say we are moving into an era when individual leadership is being replaced with group leadership. According to Max DePree, "The measure of leadership is not the quality of the head but the tone of the body. The signs of outstanding leadership appear primarily among the followers."[2] As the team develops, the ego vanishes. Paul exhorted us to lay aside our egos for the sake of the whole:

> Therefore, if there is any consolation in Christ, if any comfort of love, if any fellowship of the Spirit, if any affection and mercy, fulfill my joy by being like-minded, having the same love, being of one accord, of one mind. Let nothing be done through selfish ambition or conceit, but in lowliness of mind let each esteem others better than himself. Let each of you look out not only for his own interests, but also for the interests of others (Philippians 2:1-4, *NKJV*).

Every effective team has a strong leader. An important task of the leader (senior pastor or someone else in primary leadership), is to choose the right members to serve on the team. The many generations that make up the churches today are asking unique questions. Answering their questions and ministering to their needs, while moving the organization toward the goal the team has set, is a challenge for leadership. In his book, *Empowered Leaders,* Hans Finzel offers a list of suggested questions he uses when recruiting members for the leadership staff.

Leadership Team Interview Questions

1. Do you share a passion for our mission statement? Are we headed in the same direction? Do you understand our mission and vision, and do you buy into it with your whole heart?
2. Are we on the same page doctrinally? If you do not share the same Biblical convictions, you will have trouble as a team.
3. Are you committed to growth? Is growth a high value for you? Are you open to abandoning the status quo when necessary?
4. Do you complement the team with your gifts? Can your natural abilities and spiritual gifts make a unique contribution to the team?
5. Will you be a team player? What do you understand to be the meaning of the word *team*? Are you a loner, or are you committed to being a part of the community of leadership?

6. Do you hold to our leadership code of conduct? How do your values and convictions compare with those of our organization?
7. Do you get along well with people? What conflicts have you faced with others, and how were they resolved?
8. Are you fun to work with? Can you laugh at yourself and others? Do you enjoy working with others?
9. Do you have a track record of success? What contributions have you made in other areas of work or ministry?
10. Can you handle evaluation and correction? Can you take constructive criticism? Or do you blow up when criticized? Are you willing to be subject to an annual review, which may include both positive and negative feedback?
11. Are there embarrassing moments in your past? Is there anything in your past that if made public would be an embarrassment to you and a liability to our team?
12. Is your spouse in agreement with this decision? Is your husband or wife enthusiastic about your filling this position? Does your mate want to make this change, and will he or she support you in this new endeavor?

Every leadership team needs variety. It is counterproductive to select individuals for the team who are simply a copy of each other. Variety becomes the strength of the team. The strengths and weaknesses of individual members complement one another and fulfill Paul's exhortation to actively fulfill each member's role in the body. The common mission and each member's commitment to that mission binds the team together. Then, when differences arise, the overall purpose of the leadership team will not be threatened. Rather, mutual respect and mutual values will hold the team together.

Passing On the Faith

Even though today's leaders come from different molds with different philosophical backgrounds, church leaders must continue to build, shape and establish leaders that will uphold and maintain the standard of faith. Paul exemplified the priority of passing the faith along in Philippians 4:8, 9. He modeled the mentoring style of leadership in building his team workers.

Pastors and leaders can prepare future leaders by permitting those with leadership potential to serve with them. This means outlining the principles they teach and believe. Paul lived what he believed.

> So whether you eat or drink or whatever you do, do it all for the glory of God. Do not cause anyone to stumble, whether Jews, Greeks or the church of God—even as I try to please everybody in every way. For I am not seeking my own good but the good of many, so that they may be saved. Follow my example, as I follow the example of Christ. I praise you for remembering me in everything and for holding

> to the teachings, just as I passed them on to you" (1 Corinthians 10:31—11:2).

This style of vulnerable and servant leadership will empower others on the team.

Unity on the team must be preserved at all costs. Satan will do everything within his power to divide the team through interpersonal conflict and strife. Smart leaders recognize Satan's devices and overcome them by . . .

1. Praying together
2. Communicating and expressing concerns in a nonthreatening environment
3. Striving to live in harmony.

Keeping egos in check so that all team members understand the importance of working cooperatively toward common goals is a challenge for any leader. Problems arise when team members begin to operate on their own. Problems also arise when team members fail to identify with the vision and goals of the leader. Everyone must have a common vision, mission and goal. All must seek the Lord to know His purpose for the whole body. Most strife results when team members usurp God's will. Keeping the team unified will produce a great harvest.

One of the reasons for the fall of communism was a failure to consent to private ownership. Consequently, there was no incentive for personal productivity. Old-fashioned leaders who used power and control to lead are a dying breed.

Jesus didn't model this style of leadership. He taught servant leadership. Transformational leaders receive authority from their followers. Contemporary leadership theory envisions authority flowing upward—from followers and believers to leaders. Modern CEO's invert the organizational chart—placing the CEO on the bottom. Some church leaders have misinterpreted power for leadership. Power forces others to submit, but authority brings submission because the people want to give it.

Nebuchadnezzar exercised power when he built the golden idol for the people to worship. They bowed down because the people accepted his theory of leadership. The Hebrew boys understood it in a different light and chose to submit to God rather than the king. Leaders must earn authority, which is comprised of trust and confidence. They should realize that it is not a position, diploma, education or title that gives them the authority to lead. Those who choose to believe otherwise fail because they don't understand this principle.

Jesus, the perfect example of leadership, did not command authority. Through His servanthood, His followers chose to give Him the authority to lead. Effective leaders will follow the practice of Jesus, adopting His leadership style of humility when He washed the feet of His disciples. For a generation looking for authenticity, this could be the end to their search.

Equipping Leaders

In a lonely society that is searching for a place to belong, a leadership team that operates with a servanthood philosophy will win them. For followers to grow and become productive, members of the leadership team will need to be given authority and ownership over some part of their work. Effective leaders will not find it necessary to continue looking over everyone's shoulders. Instead, they free individual team members to work independently with the common goal in mind.

When it came time for Jesus to return to heaven, He had not spread Christianity around the world. Instead, He selected and trained 12 apostles to continue and fulfill what He had begun. That is the extreme illustration of delegation. That is what leaders today must do—establish a team to carry out their common purposes, thereby equipping leadership for the next generation.

Effective team leaders understand and appreciate the role of everyone on the team—in the nursery, in Sunday school classes and in the midweek service. Others serve as ushers or greeters, as custodians or drivers of the church bus. The effective leader will instill in the team the understanding that every person is valuable and necessary.

There's a story of a farmer who was sitting on his porch when a highway department truck pulled up along the side of the road. The farmer watched as a man got out of the truck and dug a hole. He got back into the truck and another guy got out of the truck, filled up the hole and tapped the dirt down with his foot. He got back into the truck, drove forward about 50 feet, and repeated the process. They did this four or five times. Finally the farmer could stand it no longer. He asked them what they were doing. One of the workers responded, "It's simple.

We're on a highway-beautification project, and the guy who plants the trees is out sick today."

What is the point? Everyone on the team has a role to perform. All the members of the team have been equipped to win. As the team moves in the direction God is leading, it can expect success. The difference between playing to win and playing not to lose is the difference between success and mediocrity. The following poem by an unknown author illustrates the leader who never takes a risk.

> There was a very cautious man
> Who never laughed or played.
> He never risked, he never tried.
> He never sang or prayed.
> And when he one day passed away,
> His insurance was denied.
> For since he never really lived,
> They claimed he never died.

The generations we are serving and reaching want to belong to a movement that promises success; they don't like being mediocre.

The members of the next generation will assume leadership positions in the church. For some, that's a scary thought. However, transformational leaders will accept the challenge of training them and paving the way before them. The important thing is to involve them on the team now. They can make a significant contribution. Only then can we provide opportunities for building bridges between the generations.

After World War II, there was a generation of leaders who had tremendous influence. Bill Bright of Campus Crusade for Christ, Stuart and Jill Briscoe, Billy Graham, and others made a significant impact on Christianity. However, the members of the Boomer generation have left a void in this type of visionary leadership. The Boomers basically have carried out the vision of the leaders who came before them. Leaders today must cautiously evaluate their standard of leadership as they arm the next generation of leaders.

In summary, team-based leadership and ministry is a growing movement that is changing the way churches conduct ministry. The old approach of leadership that was characterized by structure and hierarchy immobilizes members of the present generations. Often the most talented and gifted individuals are overlooked. Moving leadership to the congregation will empower these individuals and remove their limitations.

We cannot understand the importance for each team member to have an authentic relationship with God. This will supersede the priorities of professionalism and credentials of their achievement-oriented culture.

Team leadership frees the pastor from being and doing the impossible to meet the high expectations of the laity. The pastoral role will no longer be fixed, but it will be determined by his gifts, calling and the needs of the congregation. With team leadership, the congregation understands that the pastor is not the only player on the team. His role is not determined by his title—it is determined by his God-given abilities.

As you evaluate the use of teamwork in your ministry, understand the importance of hearing from God. When the children of Israel followed Moses, it wasn't because he was the perfect leader with a good idea. They believed that he had heard from God.

So if I, the Master and Teacher, washed your feet, you must now wash each other's feet. I've laid down a pattern for you. What I've done, you do. I'm only pointing out the obvious. A servant is not ranked above his master; an employee doesn't give orders to the employer. If you understand what I'm telling you, act like it—and live a blessed life

(John 13:14-17, *TM*).

We cannot do our changing alone or assume that others will wait for us to catch up. Everyone is in motion. Each church member is changing while the church is changing while the society is changing. Change is not the choice. How we handle it is.

Leith Anderson, *Dying for Change*

Changing Roles in the Family

9

And God blessed them, and God said unto them, Be fruitful, and multiply.

Genesis 1:28, KJV

At Creation, God instituted the family when He set in motion His plan for fellowship and communion. However, when mankind was given free will, he started the ball of change rolling with temptation that led to the subsequent Fall. Since that time, society has dealt with the moral decline that directly affects the family unit.

The changes impacting families today are felt worldwide. Jealousy, infidelity, conflicting values in child rearing, intergenerational conflict, alcoholism, sex, divorce, family violence, teenage pregnancies, incest and conflicts over everyday responsibilities are examples of the problems facing families today. What ever happened to the Cleavers, *Father Knows Best*, and Ozzie and Harriet?

The Church's Changing Role

Through the years, the church has created a program of ministry that has placed parents on the sidelines. They often assume the role of cheerleader or spectator, while Sunday school teachers, youth pastors and others act as coaches and team players in the spiritual formation of children. Rather than training the parents for their role of passing the faith to the next generation, the church accepted the task and bypassed the strategy God established. Through the years, the church has assumed the role of trainer. The goal of the local church should be to assist parents in their task of shaping the faith of their children. The church is a vehicle to serve the family in fulfilling their task.

To change issues, we must change the ministry. To accomplish this, we need a new strategy that focuses on changing family units. We cannot do things the way we've always done them and expect the same results!

It doesn't take a prophet to see that there will be more fragmented families, more hurting people and more psychologically scarred young people in the future. In a society where parents are working more hours in order to maintain their preferred lifestyle, family life is suffering. What used to be considered important is no longer a priority. For example, how many families in your church sit down for even one meal together each day? How many families have even periodic devotional and family nurturing times? Or, how many families attend church together, drive in one vehicle and sit together in the church services? As the family of God, what are we doing to effectively minister to these families who are forced to deal with the following aspects of society:

- Changing definition and nature of the family
- Moral decline
- Humanistic philosophy and instruction
- Secularization
- An increasing negative attitude toward children
- Abortion
- An increasing number of hurting people

We have a tremendous challenge. Deuteronomy exhorts us to pass the faith from one generation to the next. The church has done a poor job in training and equipping parents for the responsibility mandated in Deuteronomy 6:6, 7:

> Keep these words that I am commanding you today in your heart. Recite them to your children and talk about them when you are at home and when you are away, when you lie down and when you rise (*NRSV*).

A number of surveys reveal that parents have the greatest influence on their children. If that is the case, the primary role of the church is to train and encourage parents to fulfill their responsibility. In the Effective Christian Education Study conducted by Merton Strommen and Search Institute, youth whose parents maintain the tradition of religious practices in the home were compared with youth whose parents did not have an active family faith. They learned that the participation of youth coming from religious homes nearly doubled. This included participation in the church youth group, attendance at church programs and attendance at church camps. Perhaps the most important finding was that children raised in church regarded their religious faith as a very important influence in their lives. It is evident that young people who are raised in homes where faith was part of the of family life are more likely to mature in faith.

Our Response to Change in the Family

How should we respond? First of all, we need to understand the importance of relationships. As role models, parents must set a positive tone and atmosphere in the home. Stressful jobs and daily difficulties create home environments that are troubled. Positive communication does not just happen. It takes work. If children hear only derogatory remarks and harsh attitudes, their observation is that their parents do not get along. Their friends often come from divorced homes. So when they hear troubled parents, they expect divorce and separation in their home. In time, this creates fear and stress in young people's lives.

The church must respond by training parents in the skills of relationship building. This can be done through Bible studies, small-group interaction, marriage conferences and retreats. When planning these events, however, careful thought must be given to include single-parent homes as well. Blended families are becoming common. Each family unit will have its own unique issues, but all need opportunities to build relationships. It is a foundation upon which other needs can be addressed. Just as unity is necessary in the church, it is necessary in the family. As we encourage and build family unity, we enhance the building of unity in the body.

According to *USA Weekend*, April 26-28, 1996, in America today . . .

- Parents spend 40 percent less time with their children than parents of the '50s.
- Twice as many kids live in single-parent families as in the '70s.
- The average couple spends only 20 minutes a day together.
- By the time children are in junior high school, they have seen 8,000 murders on television.
- One parent in eight abuses alcohol.
- One teen in three has sex by the time they reach the eighth grade.

While many church groups may not have a high number of nontraditional family groups, there is a greater number of blended families and single-parent families than ever before.

High stress results when both parents work outside the home, when there is a breakdown of the traditional family unit, when there are highly mobile families, and where there is a high incident of substance abuse by youth. Separation from extended family members creates further stress. Their aloneness brings even greater stress.

Ministry that understands the real needs of families will flourish. Ministry teams must reach hurting family members and help them build better relationships. The church's participation will bring meaningful connections among family members, as well as between the family and the church.

The family unit changes daily. Many church leaders continue to utilize programs and ministries that are no longer relevant. Although the church supposedly stands for family unity, the truth is that the church often becomes as much a factor of dividing the family as does society.

Ministry Evaluation

Consider the following questions for evaluation in your approach to ministry:

- Are children, teens and adults utilized in the worship service?
- Does your church offer intergenerational activities and programming in its structure?

- Does the praise and worship appeal to only those individuals who were born before 1970?
- Is there an opportunity to "showcase" the families who are active in your church?
- Does your structure and program allow for single-parent families to be involved without feeling out of place?

Suggestions for Family Ministry Effectiveness

The following ideas will enhance family focus in your ministry.

1. Design and develop creative ministry communication with the family in mind. In your church bulletin, newsletter and other promotionals, include various family images, including all races.
2. Provide alternative worship schedules. Today's lifestyles do not always coincide with a highly structured worship time at exactly 10:50 a.m. on Sunday morning. Develop variety in style and format. Be flexible! Consider an intergenerational approach to worship, using various age groups.
3. Consider the real needs of the families in your community. Conduct a survey to determine the needs. Consider providing counseling services, financial management classes and other pertinent programs.

4. Offer activities that allow for substitute family members. We live in a transient society. The high divorce rate, dysfunctional family units, blended families and diversified careers require families to move often. No longer do we see the extended family unit in a single community or church. These same transient family members are looking for a place to belong, a place to be accepted, and a place to serve. The church can provide all these. Small groups can offer opportunities to build relationships. Substitute grandparents can help children who are separated from their own grandparents. "Big-Brother" and "Big-Sister" programs can assist single parents.

5. Evaluate the needs for social interaction. Parents need help with their children's education. Tutoring ministry is an option for many churches, either in a convenient church location or in a housing complex to reach out to the community.

6. Ministry to single-parent families is necessary today. Thirty-two percent of all children in the United States live in a single-parent family. These single-adult parents need support, encouragement, education, financial assistance and friendship. Activities that involve their children are appreciated. Support groups for divorced parents demonstrate to the community a nonjudgmental attitude and provide an atmosphere of love and acceptance. Practical help with household chores illustrates a loving and caring heart.

7. Parents want to be in a church where people know them and their children by name and show them attention. Send mail to the children. The parents will realize that you truly care.
8. Communicate the church ministries, programs, and structure with the parents. Include parents in the planning by offering training programs to help them raise godly children.
9. Schedule family nights throughout the year. Activities could include watching a movie together, creating decorations for shut-ins, participating in seasonal activities, and other family activities.
10. Schedule an open house at your church to invite family members to walk through the church facilities and meet the individuals who minister to the children, teens and other family members. Exhibits can also be set up to display the ministries in the local church.
11. Intergenerational Sunday school classes provide opportunities for parents and children to interact together in a small-group setting. The church provides parents with the teaching materials and they in turn lead their family in study.
12. A "Parent of the Week" program that features a different parent each week will help staff become more familiar with parents. It also helps other students become familiar with the parents of their classmates. Princeton Pike

Church of God in Hamilton, Ohio, has incorporated a "Family of the Month" program. Each month the family's name is announced in service and in the church newsletter and bulletin. This could be further emphasized by reserving a parking spot for the family and introducing them to the congregation.

13. Include children in the worship service. This announces to the congregation that you value the children and believe they can make a contribution to the church ministry. Families could also be featured together in the service, with Scripture reading, prayer and involvement on the praise and worship team.

14. Families can serve together as greeters and ushers.

15. Create professional "child-friendly" facilities in the church that conveys your love for children.

16. Provide the resources families needed to do their job. Do they need help with a strong-willed child? Are they having difficulty understanding their teen? Gather resources to make available when the need arises.

17. Evaluate the possibility of appointing a minister to families for your church leadership team.

Paradigm Shift

Have you noticed how many fathers are now staying at home while mothers go to work? Many hotels are promoting "getaway packages" that provide activities for the entire family. The popularity of mini-vans for families, home-schooling and free kids meals are all part of a paradigm shift relating to the family and the church. The former model was one in which the home supported the ministries of the church. The new model dictates that the church do all it can to support and train parents in the development of their children's faith.

Call them all together—men, women, children, and the foreigners living in your towns—so they may listen and learn to fear the Lord your God and carefully obey all the terms of this law. Do this so that your children who have not known these laws will hear them and will learn to fear the Lord your God. Do this as long as you live in the land you are crossing the Jordan to occupy

(Deuteronomy 31:12,13, *NLT*).

I believe that a part of the job God has given me to do is to create orderly change from within the church. But that change will not come unless I consider that it is *what I do*. It is my job. I am not speaking of myself as a pastor, but as an ordinary Christian in the church. Helpful change occurs only when someone has a burden to create it. It must be planned.

Michael R. Tucker, *The Church: Change or Decay*

Processing Change

10

I have become all things to all men so that by all possible means I might save some.

1 Corinthians 9:22

The following are actual statements of church members who were confronted with change:

1. "Why should we hire an associate pastor? The pastor we've got can handle the job. Besides, we don't want anyone else to preach on a regular basis. We like our pastor's preaching."

2. "What ever happened to the hymnal? I just can't get used to these new songs. I don't know

the words. And when we had songbooks, we didn't have that projector in the sanctuary."

3. "Why can't we build a new sanctuary? What's the sense of a gymnasium? I don't care if you call it a Family Center, who ever heard of having church in a gym?"

4. "I just don't understand why we need to replace the baby grand piano with an electronic keyboard. It sounds just fine to me."

5. "But we raised the money for this class and paid for the paint, carpet and chairs. We may not be as many as we used to be, but why should we change rooms?"

It is obvious that the church is experiencing change. Life requires change. Therefore, growing churches must be willing to change. Healthy churches must accept change just as we accept change in our physical bodies.

We can change our traditions without discarding our belief in the Bible. As long as we have Biblical reasons to support our practices, we must not change them. However, we are hard pressed to find Bible verses on such common traditions as Sunday school, church nurseries, altar calls, or even singing hymns. What about the practice of baptizing by immersion or by sprinkling? Have we considered if women should cover their heads in the church?

The point is that none of these things are wrong, but any attempt to change them must be evaluated in terms of changing our traditions, not our beliefs.

The society is changing and the church must also change in order to reach members of this society. Many churches die because of their unwillingness to change. They create their own language and minister only to themselves.

Planning for Change

As we plan for change, we should understand that we have the freedom to change.

- We must break out of our traditional boxes and reduce unnecessary expectations.
- We have the freedom to make mistakes, even fail, because progress involves taking risks.
- We must discontinue programs that no longer work.

There was a time in the church when it was a good idea to publicly introduce visitors during the worship service. Door-to-door visitation was an accepted method of evangelism. Recognizing individual birthdays in church was greatly anticipated. (Members looked forward to receiving their birthday pencil after dropping their pennies into the jar for the orphans.) Some churches even sang their Christian version of the birthday song.

But times have changed, so methods must change. The apostle Paul testifies that he endeavored to become all things to all men so that he might win them over. As we seek to create change, our motivation for change must be examined. Some church leaders want to be agents of change, not because of their concern for growth and change in the body of

Christ, but because they want to control people, programs, money and the political processes. A contemporary political style is emerging in many secular organizations. This style emphasizes the processes of decision making within organizations by opening these processes to everyone involved and receiving their input.

Implementing Change

The first step is to evaluate the current ministry. Do the programs match the purpose and vision of the church? Is there any program that needs to be discontinued? Is the church meeting the needs of everyone involved in the church? Surveying the congregation will reveal personal feelings regarding the present ministry, especially if the survey is anonymous. Surveys assist the leaders in understanding why individuals chose this particular, where they feel mistakes are being made and which areas of ministry need greater attention. Evaluation of the present situation is absolutely necessary in implementing change.

Deciding to change is only half the battle. The other half involves deciding what to change. Determining the lack of consistency between the church function and the church mission is accomplished through the use of surveys and open forums.

Some leaders make the mistake of initiating change simply because their personal vision and mission does not match the present congregation. Giving ownership to those who are involved and will be affected by the proposed change will guarantee a greater rate of success. Mandated changes without these procedures will inhibit the leadership's effectiveness and influence.

Create opportunities for dialogue focusing on the question, "Why?" Questioning why the ministry exists will assist in the development of a revised or new mission statement. The survey will also acknowledge and validate the opinions of the members of the congregation. Encouraging frank responses without repercussion will reveal new areas of need. Sometimes perceptions are not accurate in some ministry areas. Having an open mind is necessary for this process to succeed. Defensive attitudes discourage honest responses. And without honest responses, true evaluation is not possible. The three basic questions for evaluation include the following:

- What are we doing?
- What do we want to change?
- How can we accomplish the change?

By responding to these questions, the participants can formulate a statement of purpose. Sowing seeds of discontent about the present state of church life will lead to a desire to leave the present—even though it appears risky—and make room for an appealing future.

Assessing Problems

Once the current programs are evaluated, then the remainder of the change procedure can begin. The underlying problem can be defined by looking at the results of the dialogue and survey responses. Often with relationships, some people don't work well together. Sometimes the problem is the lack of resources and facilities. Some situations might need to be remodeled, redefined, removed or rearranged. The real reason individuals will not volunteer for nursery care might be the nursery facilities. Or, it might be a conflict with an individual who heads the nursery. Churches are guilty of advancing people into leadership positions based on the success they had in other assignments. For example, good teachers don't always make good superintendents. A faithful and talented choir member may not be qualified to serve as choir director. Another underlying problem in some ministries is their lack of desire to grow. Perhaps the people involved don't see a need for growth. Before change can be instituted, all the underlying problems must be identified.

In order to change, the power structure must be uncovered and dismantled. John Maxwell has said that true leaders know how to influence the influencers. Usually the power structure consists of workers who have long tenure. And since power people often do not have a high visibility, the one trying to create change will need to determine where the real power lies.

Next, the people must be educated at all levels of administration. This means doing your homework. Then, slowly educate the leaders without manipulating them to your point of view. Bounce ideas off different people. Ask for honest evaluation. Be willing for your ideas to die a quick death. Sometimes leaders are wrong! And there is always wisdom in the counsel of many.

Evaluating the Feedback

The tough part of change involves evaluating feedback. Comments like the following must be cautiously evaluated:

- "No one likes the new Sunday school curriculum."
- "The music is too loud."
- "We don't understand those songs."
- "Everybody thinks the new youth pastor is doing his job poorly."
- "She shouldn't be allowed to sing solos again. Her style doesn't fit here."
- "The new schedule is a stupid idea."

Don't accept one or two complaints. Even feedback from those in power is not always a true reading. Find the original source. Gather all the facts from a cross-section of people before responding.

Only after evaluating the feedback can you begin to set new goals. You want to create order from within, explaining what you expect to accomplish with the proposed change. Because goal setting keeps leaders on track, it must involve various groups in the church. Many ministries conduct annual planning sessions to evaluate and study the previous year's accomplishments. During these planning sessions, changes will be contemplated with less resistance. As the staff and leadership consider God's will for the ministry, they can ask the question, "What does God want our ministry to be in three years, four years, or 10 years?" By specifying the time factor, leaders can be more specific in defining their plans and strategy in each area of the ministry involved. The discrepancies that surface provide opportunities to discuss needed changes. Long-term and short-term goals will need to be set for each area analyzed. Present each change as a way to reach the agreed-upon goals.

As observations and responses are calculated, a style of leadership must be adopted. Various seasons in the church require different styles of leading. Keeping the idea of change fresh in the minds of the congregation is valuable. We all like to see movement and progress. If changes just slip by quietly, some people will not notice. For example, a little creativity in the morning worship service on Sunday can demonstrate to the congregation the message, "We are open to change in this church." When the choir gets new robes or changes places when they sing, talking about it will create a climate for further change. Demonstrating how the church is already involved in change may help those who fear change to see they only fear certain changes. In sharing dreams, vision, and goals for change, leaders must use tact and diplomacy. Care must also be taken in relating planned changes. In an effort to encourage ownership, there are occasions when it is better to allow the influencers to broadcast the vision. Younger members must exercise even more caution because people are often intimidated, and even offended, by the "new kid on the block."

Leaders and organizers of the future must be flexible in their response. Generation X, as well as the Millennial generation that follows, will need to be led differently than those in previous generations.

Niccolo Machiavelli, one of the first writers on leadership, wrote *The Prince*, in 1532. He observed, "There is nothing more difficult to handle, more doubtful of success, nor more dangerous to manage, than to put oneself at the head of introducing new orders. For the introducer has all those who benefit from the old orders as enemies, and he has lukewarm defenders in all those who might benefit from the new orders." Leadership must manage change. Yet nothing is more hazardous to a leader's health! It has been said that the six last words of the church are, "We've always done it that way!"

In the process of leading change, we must understand and educate the people to the vast difference between theology and methodology. Our doctrines are inspired by God and are permanent; however, as times change, our methods must change with them. The apostle Paul understood the necessity of change when he wrote 1 Corinthians 9:19-23. He realized that he had to adapt to different audiences:

> For though I am free from all men, I have made myself a servant to all, that I might win the more; and to the Jews I became as a Jew, that I might win Jews; to those who are under the law, as under the law, that I might win those who are under the law; to those who are without law, as without law (not being without law toward God, but under law toward Christ), that I might win those who are without law; to the weak I became as weak, that I might win the weak. I have become all things

> to all men, that I might by all means save some. Now this I do for the gospel's sake, that I may be partaker of it with you.

It is our responsibility to teach the differences between values (our preferences) and beliefs (our moral absolutes). Every issue is not worth a fight. This places priority on the major issues and assists the leaders in facing changes head-on.

Why change? The following reasons should be considered:

- God wants to do a new thing. He is stirring the hearts of the members.
- The ministry is plateaued—just the same old thing.
- There is a lack of volunteers, financial growth and involvement of the body.
- There is a constant turnover; people are exiting through the back door.
- Cultural shifts create a new climate for change.
- No one seems to know where the ministry is going—there are no goals and objectives.
- The workforce reveals that changes are needed in our priorities, demographics and morale.

Current Trends

Hans Finzel, in his book *Empowered Leaders,* refers to Pastor Leith Anderson and a message he presented in a seminary chapel. Anderson spoke of ministry trends that reflect significant change in values from previous decades. Among those mentioned are listed here:

- Effectiveness has joined faithfulness as a measurement for successful ministry.
- Godliness is necessary for ministry today.
- Learning is a lifelong process for ministers.
- Relationships are a key motivation for people going to church, rather than good preaching.
- Much information is available for church leaders.
- Mega churches, conferences and seminars have surpassed denominations and seminaries in influence.
- Programs have become more important than preaching.
- Ministry teams have become the model for effective leadership.[1]

Expectations of leaders are rising. These changing expectations rest not only in the church, but in all avenues of culture. People in general have become more critical of leaders and changing rules. This lessens the pool of prospective leaders to assume the role of leadership.

As the church moves through its life cycle, there will be fruitful seasons of change in the body. These seasons will provide an open climate for accepting change. The Church of God in Milford, Ohio, dealt with change after the sudden death of my dad in January 1999. He had served as pastor of this congregation for over 10 years, which is considered by some to be a long-term pastorate. His death precipitated a crisis. The people were accustomed to my dad's leadership style. They had followed his vision and enjoyed the stability of his leadership over the years. I am sure some would have liked to see changes, but out of respect for his godly leadership, they chose not to introduce them.

Change was inevitable. The new pastor selected by the congregation was much younger. He came to the church with a vision from God. As was expected, there were changes, and the congregation was more open than they might have been prior to the pastoral change. The new pastor respected the former pastor's leadership and began to build on what had been accomplished. In fact, he compared my dad to Moses and himself to Joshua. The changes he introduced were in addition to what had been done, not a substitute or even a replacement. The effective agent of change understands the necessity of doing this.

Fear of Discarding the Past

People resist change because they fear discarding the past, rather than discovering the future. Leaders who have new appointments gain the respect of their coworkers if they understand this principle. God does not require the destruction of everything and everyone that has come before to use you in a new ministry. Even if the predecessor failed, he will still be perceived by some as a good leader. He had a positive influence on some who will resist the changes presented by new leadership because they don't want to switch loyalties. God still has a plan, and crises situations sometimes enhance the openness to His new plan.

I recall the time at the South Aurora Church of God in Aurora, Illinois, when the church and community faced a crisis in the school system. My dad led the congregation in a time of prayer and evaluation to find a solution for this deplorable situation. Through the leading of God and their sensitivity of the leadership toward their mission, the church opened a Christian day school. The crisis led to this major change. It effected everything—the facilities, personnel, church schedule and the overall philosophy of the church ministry. Relying on God's voice and obediently following His leading, the community and church experienced a great harvest, even though it was a major change for their ministry.

I heard about a pastor who had a burden for the inner city of the metropolitan area where his church was located. To share this vision with the congregation, he arranged a tour of the inner city. Many in the congregation had no idea of the living conditions of the people in their community. The pastor gave them the opportunity to see the need firsthand. As a result, the congregation responded to this new vision and what they believed God wanted them to do.

In my own leadership experience, I have detected opportunities for change when accepting a new leadership position. Whether it be the pastorate, an administrative office or teaching a class, those in my care often expressed concern about the future of the ministry. Their concern opened up dialogue so that the vision could be shared.

Examples of Effective Change

When I accepted the pastorate of the South Park Church in Council Bluffs, Iowa, I stepped into a difficult situation. The property was for sale, the church and the parsonage needed repair, the congregation had split, and finances were at an all-time low. The former pastor had done an excellent job caring for and loving the people, following the fall of the previous pastor. After boosting the morale of the people, it became my lot to start the rebuilding process. The church was definitely open to change. As we began discussing the future goals of the church, a new vision was born. This leadership change had opened the door for change.

Accepting the appointment to serve as state director of youth and Christian education for the Church of God in Southern Ohio was a new area of ministry for me. I immediately recognized the need for change in several areas. This is not a negative reflection of my predecessor—it is a reflection of a different philosophy of ministry that came in a ripe season of change in the ministry I was leading. When overseeing the youth camps, my administrative style was different. While training the staff, I began to circulate the phrase "Change is good." As I walked around the campground, I would hear my statement repeated. Slowly, they began to cooperate as I explained the motivation behind the changes the supervising board and I had initiated. When they understood our reasoning, the entire staff claimed ownership of the process and change became effective.

My dad often told me that people should not be approached about a conflict or a proposed change until God had a chance to work in their lives. He was a man of prayer and understood the power of prayer. It was his opinion that if a leader could get the people on their knees, he would see a more unified and cooperative body that would listen to the voice of God and obey His leading. After times of refreshing sent by God, either in a regular service or after a revival, he would sow the seeds of change in the lives of the decision makers in the congregation. He had greater success in implementing change by waiting for God to move. He realized that as a leader, he could also be wrong at times. Therefore, a slower response would allow time for God to speak to him as well.

In conclusion, the change process is often slow and hazardous. However, we can rest in the assurance that God has a plan and purpose for every ministry. He had a plan and a future for each ministry He set in motion. When implementing change, we cannot forget the past. Rather, we must look at the significant happenings and moving of God as He worked out His plan in the life of the ministry. This requires building on the successes of the past, seeking godly counsel for the future and sharing the vision with the people. Implement the change and believe God for a fruitful harvest.

"For I know the thoughts that I think toward you," says the Lord, "thoughts of peace and not of evil, to give you a future and a hope"
(Jeremiah 29:11, *NKJV*).

Very few people begin life saying, "I want to change the world." Even people who have left an undeniable mark on this world rarely set out to make that difference. Yet there are windows of time in one's life when one has the power to change things. These times are pivotal points. At our moment of decision we can drift back into the doldrums or march boldly into the future.

Rick Ezell, *Ministry on the Cutting Edge*

Epilogue

Revelation 14:14-16, NKJV

Then I looked, and behold, a white cloud, and on the cloud sat One like the Son of Man, having on His head a golden crown, and in His hand a sharp sickle. And another angel came out of the temple, crying with a loud voice to Him who sat on the cloud, "Thrust in Your sickle and reap, for the time has come for You to reap, for the harvest of the earth is ripe." So He who sat on the cloud thrust in His sickle on the earth, and the earth was reaped.

In His hand, He holds a sharp sickle. The time has come to reap. Jesus is the Lord of the harvest. We can say that the Lord of the harvest has an instrument in His hand. You and I are His instrument of harvest. This is harvest time and the best is before us!

Sharp Instruments

God only uses sharp instruments in reaping the harvest. We need to examine our ministry and ask,

"Have we lost our cutting edge?" For maximum effectiveness in this changing society, it is imperative for the Holy Spirit to anoint us. God isn't looking only for those with great abilities, tremendous talent, or gifts—He uses ordinary people to reap the harvest. We see many individuals in Scripture who were not perfect.

- Abraham was too old.
- David was too young.
- Moses stuttered.
- Elijah was depressed.
- Jonah ran from God.
- Noah got drunk.
- Jacob was deceitful.
- David was an adulterer and a murderer.
- John the Baptist was too stern.
- Martha was a worrier.
- James and John wanted to call down fire from heaven.
- Peter was afraid of death.
- Thomas doubted.

The list is endless when we evaluate why people should not have been used by God. However, God used them because they were on the cutting edge; they were anointed. If God could use all these people in Scripture, there is certainly hope for us.

Ecclesiastes 10:10 reminds us that more strength is needed if the edge is dull. The Bible is filled with success stories. God did not create us to fail. In the midst of changes, ministry can be frustrating. However, Christ didn't establish His church to fail either. He raised up churches to win the harvest for Christ.

The generations we are working with are not looking for dull Christians who make God sound boring. The harvest will only be reaped by those who are empowered by the Holy Spirit.

Changes can sometimes be confusing and frustrating. When there are different expectations, many times we don't believe our contributions are making a difference. The challenge then is to stop and check our cutting edge. Has it lost its effectiveness? If so, the cutting edge requires fresh oil and a fresh anointing.

The Lost Cutting Edge

In 2 Kings 6, the story is told about a young woodcutter who found himself standing before the task without his cutting edge and the prophet Elisha helped him find it. "But as one was cutting down a tree, the iron ax head fell into the water; and he cried out and said, 'Alas, master! For it was borrowed.' So the man of God said, 'Where did it fall?' And he showed him the place. So he cut off a stick, and threw it in there; and he made the iron float. Therefore he said, 'Pick it up for yourself.' So he reached out his hand and took it" (vv. 5-7, *NKJV*).

The woodcutter had the handle, but the effectiveness had been removed. That is where many Christians are today. They don't have what they need to be effective, to teach their class of sixth-grade boys, or face the challenge of sickness and disease.

Recovering the Cutting Edge

1. *Ask the right questions.* In verse 6, the man of God said, "Where did it fall?" We need to ask ourselves the same question. The business of every Christian believer is to reach every lost person with the gospel of Jesus Christ. Is it possible that the reason we lost our cutting edge is that we no longer have a passion for the lost? Jesus came to call the sinners, not the righteous, to repentance. Since we are experiencing so many changes, it is imperative to identify how to get back to the basics of evangelism in our ministry. Our methodology may need to change as we target the harvest. The sharp edge may require us to do things differently than ever before. We must be willing to do whatever is necessary in order to win the lost. We must ask God what He would have us do.

2. *You cannot recover the cutting edge alone.* Proverbs 27:17 tells us that iron sharpens iron. We all need three types of people in our lives: a mentor like Paul who has gone before us; a peer like Barnabas who loves us and is loyal to us (but who is not impressed with us); and a disciple like Timothy to train to be like Christ. In order to keep us sharp, these individuals must love us enough to tell us when we're wrong.

3. *Be open to God's unique plan for your life.* The Bible records that Elisha threw a stick in the water. We must be careful to understand that each ministry is different, each harvest field unique. Saturday

Sunday school may work in some communities. In others, Sunday night Sunday school may be more profitable. And still in others, the traditional Sunday morning Sunday school may be the best strategy. The key is to recognize your uniqueness and understand that God has a specific plan and mission for every harvest field. Are you open to His plan, even though you may have never done it that way before? When we stand before God, all He will require is that we be found faithful using the gifts He has given us.

4. *Ask God for a supernatural experience to bring your cutting edge back to the surface.* Ax heads don't swim, but the Bible records that the ax head rose to the surface and began to float. With God, all things are possible. The harvest may look impossible to reach, but God reminds us that He is able to do all things. We must depend on Him, not ourselves. He is a creative God. Just look in the mirror and examine His creative ability. He has ideas for us to utilize in our ministries that we have never considered. The secret is to discover His plan and vision for our ministry.

5. *How do you recover the cutting edge?* The *New King James Version* says, "Pick it up for yourself." Those individuals with passion will move from devotion to action. The violent take it by force. It's time for believers to reach out and take the cutting edge God is sending their way. He is moving supernaturally to reach the harvest. The Lord of the harvest with a sickle in His hand says to us, the church: I want to restore the cutting edge because the time of the harvest is now!

In his book, *The Secret of Christian Joy,* Vance Havner refers to the story about the ax head. He says, "Many of the Lord's workmen today have lost the ax head of power. They have lost the joy of salvation, they have not the upholding of God's Spirit. The lost ax head of the Spirit's unction has fallen into the waters of worldliness, ponds of indifference, swamps of sluggishness. They have ability, training, sincerity, earnestness, but they are chopping with the handle. They stand before a demonized world powerless, and it must be said of them, as it was said of the disciples before the demon-possessed boy, 'and they could not . . . '(Mark 9:18). The pitiful tragedy of the lost ax heads in the church today!"[1]

The disciples of the early church ministered effectively because they were infused with God's power. The same power is available to us when we tap into God's resources. God has equipped us with energy and gifts to reap the harvest, in spite of the changes we encounter. However, in order to be effective, we will be required to dream dreams, take risks and utilize the power He provides.

It's up to you. Will you continue doing business as usual, while the world with all its changes passes you by? Or will you change your world? You have the option of living on the dull edge of apathy, fear, complacency, status quo and tradition, or you can seek God, hear His voice and minister on the cutting edge. It's time to make a difference—march into unchartered territories, color outside the lines! Only when we dare to be different can we make a difference. You must not only desire change, but you must also create change by making things happen. The choice is yours. The time is now!

Notes

Chapter 1

[1]*Youthworker Journal*, bi-monthly publication of CCM (Jan./Feb. 2000) 27.

Chapter 2

[1]George Barna, *Second Coming of the Church* (Nashville: Word, 1998) 93.

Chapter 3

[1]William J. Bennett, *The Index of Leading Cultural Indicators* (Colorado Springs: Waterbrook, 1999) 57.

[2]Bennett, several areas of the book.

[3]Shelly Cunningham, "Children's Ministry in Changing Times," *Sundoulos* (Summer 1992).

[4]Bennett, 151.

[5]David Middlebrook, *Ministries Today* (Jan./Feb. 2000).

Chapter 8

[1]Wayne Rice, *Hot Illustrations for Youth Talks* (Grand Rapids: Zondervan, 1994) 120, 121.

[2]Max DePree, *Leadership Is an Art* (New York: Dell, 1989) 14.

Chapter 10

[1]Hans Finzel, *Empowered Leaders*, sermon, Leith Anderson, "Ministry:Not the Same Yesterday, Today and Forever," Bethel Seminary, St. Paul, MN, 1 Jan. 1996 (Nashville:Word, 1998) 112-113.

Epilogue

[1]Vance Havner, *The Secret of Christian Joy* (Philadelphia: Pinebrook Book Club, 1938) 58, 59.